KITCHEN TABLE TYCOON

How to make it work as a mother and an entrepreneur

Anita Naik

piatkus

PIATKUS

First published in Great Britain in 2008 by Piatkus Books
This paperback edition published in 2010 by Piatkus

A CIP catalogue record for this book
is available from the British Library.

ISBN 978-0-7499-2945-9

Text design by Goldust Design
Edited by Jan Cutler
Typeset in Bembo by Goldust Design
Printed and bound in Great Britain by
CPI Mackays, Chatham ME5 8TD

Papers used by Piatkus are natural, renewable and recyclable
products sourced from well-managed forests and certified
in accordance with the rules of the Forest Stewardship Council.

Piatkus
An imprint of
Little, Brown Book Group
100 Victoria Embankment
London EC4Y 0DY

An Hachette UK Company
www.hachette.co.uk

www.piatkus.co.uk

For my mother, who showed me how it was possible to have a career and be a good mum, and for my father, who showed me the spirit of entrepreneurship.

Contents

Acknowledgements

Grateful thanks to Karly Hodson who looked after Bella so that I could write this book, Judy Piatkus and Alice Davis for making working together such a pleasure, and to Joe who does the same for my home life. And a very big thank you to all the brilliant Kitchen Table Tycoons (see Appendix) who gave me their time, help, advice and stories for this book. May they inspire you to take the leap, and go for it, too.

Introduction

Fed up with the working for someone else, commuting at the crack of dawn and leaving your kids in nursery all day? Well, you're not alone, a poll carried out by workingmums.co.uk shows that 87 per cent of mums would gladly ditch the office to enjoy the benefits of working from home, whereas in the US 25 million people are already doing it. If this is your dream and you're currently mulling over creating your own business, then this is the book for you, as *Kitchen Table Tycoon* is all about how to get from those wishful thoughts to the reality of setting up your own business, literally from your kitchen table.

So what gives me the right to write this book? Aside from being a mum, I've run my own successful writing business from home for the last 16 years (writing mostly books, magazine articles, press releases and advertising copy for consumer and corporate companies), and so I know all about the ins and outs, pitfalls and highs of running a business from home. When I started I was child-free and so could put all my efforts into my business, yet I struggled with the same aspects all home starts-ups have: loneliness, cash-flow anxieties and endless business-plan rewrites. Once I had a baby, new challenges arose, such as how to work when you've had only three hours' sleep; how to work when you feel guilty; and how to work to a deadline when you can hear your child crying in another room, even though someone else is on hand to help. But I'm proof that it can be done, and what's more I know it can work fantastically well, which is why when other friends began asking me for my advice on how to do it, and also posed questions such as 'How can I find a business idea?' or 'What do I do about marketing and money?', the idea for this book was born.

However, I'm not going to lie to you. Setting up a business from scratch, never mind from home with a kid on your lap, is a daunting prospect, especially from a financial point of view, which is why many people don't do it. Let's face it, it's frightening to give up benefits such as holiday and sickness pay, not to mention a secure wage packet, but the trick is to balance what you're scared about against what you'll gain by working for yourself.

For me this means getting to be my own boss and calling the shots both in my work and home life. Like many women I initially left my job because I was fed up. After years of working for the same employer, I wanted to branch out and write for new companies as well as adding new strings to my bow, such as becoming an author, writing copy for corporate companies, and even doing some work in television. Apart from these ambitions, I was also sick of commuting, and I wanted to be my own boss, despite the fact that I had no idea how to start a business, run a business or even plan for a successful business.

Thankfully, I've managed to do all of the above. However, when I became a mum I had to reinvent myself again. Gone were the days when I could work from 7.00 am to 7.00 pm or take the afternoons off, and gone were the nights where I would willingly stay up to finish writing a book.

I may have moaned about the tribulations of working for myself when I was childless but the second I became a mum life became a bit of a multitasking nightmare. Apart from the angst of working versus childcare, and having conference calls with a baby on my lap, fatigue is my biggest enemy, and yet I still love working for myself, which is why I am a huge advocate of mums running their own businesses.

Like many of the Kitchen Table Tycoons I have interviewed for this book, I've found that the amazing upside to working from home is that not only do I get to balance my family and work life more effectively than friends who have had to go back to work but I've also been able to avoid long hours away from my baby while doing the work that I love. So, if you're tempted to set up your own business, but daunted at the prospect of juggling work, domesticity and motherhood, don't give up before you've begun. No matter how sleep deprived you are right now, or how scared you feel about throwing in your job, if having your own business is something you want to do, it's more than possible to do it.

Which is why, apart from all the business basics, this book is all about going for it, and taking an idea from the page to reality. What's more it's also about the pitfalls that every mumpreneur encounters, and how to sustain your confidence and energy when you've had three hours' sleep and no one will take your calls. So, if you feel willing to go the distance, bear in mind that by this time next year you could be a Kitchen Table Tycoon, too; meaning, the door to a better work–life balance, not to mention independence and financial security, could be just around the corner for you. So, take a deep breath and give it a go.

CHAPTER ONE

Are you a Kitchen Table Tycoon?

Let's face it, running your own business is the new global fantasy. Ask around and it seems that everybody is a wannabe entrepreneur with a great idea. Maybe you already have yours, along with a fantastic company name and an idea for a logo. Or perhaps you're playing with a couple of ideas in your head or are simply dreaming of finding a new venture and giving up your day job. Wherever you are with your dream vision, it's likely you're also wondering if running a business from home is really for you. If so, you're not alone, because even if you have the most brilliant of business ideas, starting up on your own, giving up a secure pay cheque and becoming a jack of all trades is a scary prospect. And one most likely to have you trembling with a wide variety of fears, such as fear of failure, fear of financial ruin, fear you're not the business type and, top of the list, fear that you'll end up losing everything you own.

Yet, despite these universal fears, the good news is that small businesses are on the increase all over the world, with Kitchen Table Tycoons – mothers who are entrepreneurs – being one of the fastest growing sectors in this area!

So, if you're currently toying with the idea of working for

yourself but thinking there's no way you could do it now that you have kids, it's worth knowing that it's achievable. In fact, many of the mums featured throughout this book have done what many people thought impossible and balanced motherhood with a very successful home business. Some have taken a 'mum problem' and turned it into a trade, whereas others have found an amazing idea and run with it. What's more, many of these home companies aren't side projects that bring in a bit of extra pocket money but prosperous businesses that have a turnover of millions.

All of which means you're not being ridiculous, foolish or impractical just because you have kids and feel desperate to work from home. Studies show that three-quarters of women starting up businesses do so when their children are under two years old, with the number of home-based businesses in the US currently hovering at around 25 million (according to International Data Corp – IDC). What's more, according to a national survey conducted by Ipsos-Reid on behalf of Microsoft Canada, 54 per cent of female Canadian small-business owners feel that being able to work at home to raise their family was a key reason for leaving their nine-to-five jobs. In the UK, research by Dr Tim Leunig of the London School of Economics (who was the first to identify the new breed of 'Kitchen Table Tycoons') found that plenty of women are successfully juggling the roles of mother and magnate, and that:

➤ More than a third (36 per cent) of female entrepreneurs are aged between 26 and 30.

➤ Seventy-four per cent of women who started a

business did so after they gave birth or when their child was under two years old.

➤ A quarter of the women (26 per cent) started up their own business because they were frustrated working for someone else, with more than a third (38 per cent) pursuing their 'big idea' because it allowed them to juggle a career and motherhood.

➤ Three-quarters (73 per cent) of those questioned currently feel 'satisfied' or 'very satisfied', and two-thirds (66 per cent) feel more satisfied than they were in previous jobs.

➤ The founders of the global brand Taggies are the perfect example of the Kitchen Table Tycoon. Eight years ago, Julie Dix, 40, and Danielle Ayotte, 37, were stay-at-home mums, who met each other through their children's playgroup, and began not only a friendship but also a business. Their company, Taggies, is based on the idea that babies and young kids love playing with labels and tags, the idea for the product coming to Julie when she watched her own son play with a tag on an old blanket. The idea for the business grew from that into an inter-active and educational blanket trimmed with a variety of satin ribbons that babies could play with and learn from.

Whereas neither Julie nor Danielle had any business experience (Julie was an early-learning teacher and Danielle an office manager), thanks to the advice of friends and family they took a deep breath and started Taggies, and have watched their company's revenue double every year since it was founded in 1999.

In true entrepreneurial style the duo worked from home, taking orders at their kitchen tables, stacking boxes in their garages, and selling at area markets, all while trying to entertain, feed and change their kids' nappies. Their big break came in 2003 when Scholastic Books came calling, saying it wanted to set up a licensing agreement in which Scholastic would produce Taggies books, and has now sold 1.5 million since 2003. Taggies has also won numerous awards and is now a million-dollar business venture.

Like Danielle and Julie show, it pays not to give up just because you aren't a classic businessperson or because your idea seems so simple. Rather than letting fear be your guide, consider the prospect of working for yourself as the chance to be independent, successful and, hopefully, prosperous, as well as someone who, at the end of the day, can put her hand on her heart and say she feels completely happy about her work–life–motherhood balance.

Are you ready to work for yourself?

'The media image of an entrepreneur isn't correct. We're not all ruthless and perfect. In fact we all make mistakes and we all get nervous.'
Rachael Talpin, AboutMyArea and Mums In Control

The big question is, of course, where should you start, especially if you have no real idea, no business know-how and, let's be honest, no idea if you're really someone suited to

working on her own. Well, the very first step to take before
business plans, brainstorming and handing in your resignation is to be 100 per cent honest with yourself. Whereas
being your own boss and working from home is an exciting
idea, rich in financial possibilities as well as the answer to
seeing more of your kids and ending some of that mummy
guilt, the question is: are you really someone who can be a
mumpreneur and work on her own from home?

Before I started out alone from home I was a bit shaky on
this area, like many of the women interviewed for this book.
I knew I was good at the big picture – that is, I was creative
and loved the idea of working from home – but I also knew
I was bad on details such as accounting, marketing and time
management. None of these things meant that I shouldn't go
it alone, but only that I needed to beef up my weak areas if I
was going to make it work.

What's more, I was more than a bit idealistic about working
from home with a baby. I'll work when she sleeps, I originally thought, and then had a baby who didn't like to sleep.
I then thought that having a nanny to take over the childcare while I was working would be like having the best of
both worlds: I'd get to work all day and also get to see my
daughter. Well, I do get to see her all day, and unfortunately
I also get to hear her screaming for me (and not her nanny
who's trying to placate her), usually just when I am trying to
write something important or take a meeting on the phone.
Luckily my nanny is fantastic and I'm also adept at multitasking, which means if I want to I can stop work and change
nappies and/or take a work call, and write while tuning out
her screams for attention. It's not ideal, because no matter
who is with your child your instinct is to rush in, and it's not

guilt-free but it works for me and, more importantly, I know in the long run that we'll all gain from it.

These are just some of the reasons why it pays to know yourself inside out before you throw in your day job. So, if you're considering becoming a kitchen-table worker here are the questions to ask yourself:

1. Are you're someone who can motivate herself to get going, especially when you're tired, fed up and exhausted?

2. Are you capable of scraping yourself off the floor to work when things get tough on the home front?

3. Can you switch swiftly between domestic and work tasks?

4. Can you deal with the insecurity of not always being paid on time?

5. Are you able to work and not be distracted by your home life and kids?

6. Can you sort out some part-time childcare?

7. Can you cope with the isolation of working alone with no one for company?

8. Can you deal with the pressure on your own when things go wrong?

9. Are you willing to sacrifice your leisure time?

10. Can you control your finances?

11. Can you live without a guaranteed income?

12. Are you prepared to go back to basics and learn new skills?

Answer 'no' to more than two of the above and working from home is not for you, mainly because if you have kids you don't need me to tell you that being a mum can be exhausting and relentless, and if you then factor into an average child-care day a full working day with equal demands, which starts somewhere between your 5.30 am wake-up, and your kids' nap times, you'll see why it might not work for you.

'In the beginning I think I worked so hard because fear motivated me – that whisper in your ear that four out of five businesses fail in the first five years. Then letting people down – I hate to do that. Also, I am very competitive and I love to win, and business can be very much like a game, so all those things pushed me forwards.'
Janine Allis, Boost Juice

However, don't get me wrong, running your own business from home is not unachievable, and running one from home with kids around is not impossible – but before you choose to do it, it's essential that you're aware that it's not the easy option. Plus, if you think you're being pulled in two directions now, it will be even harder when you have a client on the phone demanding your full attention and your child at your door demanding the same.

So the question is: have you got what it takes? Whereas there is a variety of online tests out there where you can check whether you have the entrepreneurial spirit and drive, it's worth knowing that being a mumpreneur is different from being your average entrepreneur; meaning, these business tests aren't always great indicators of whether you're suited to working on your own. If you've tried them and scored badly, take heart – you could be like some of the Kitchen Table Tycoons in this book and find that whereas you fail every aptitude and psychometric test, you are more than able to run a viable business. This is because Kitchen Table Tycoons bring different talents to the table, so just because you aren't a run-of-the-mill version of a ruthless entrepreneur or organised to a scary level it doesn't mean that you can't do it.

'I never thought I'd be someone to ever run my own business. I failed all the tests for entrepreneurs and instead I created my business on an evolutionary basis and learned as I went along.'
Melissa Talago, Peekaboo Communications

The test below will help you to uncover whether being a mumpreneur is for you, as it takes into account all areas of your life and will help you to identify those areas that could do with a helping hand. Take each quiz separately and add up your scores, reading the answers for each area. At the end total all your scores and find out whether you have what it takes to be a Kitchen Table Tycoon.

Your life

....

1 Is your family supportive of you working for yourself?

(a) Yes (10)

(b) No (5)

(c) You haven't asked them (0)

2 Could your family survive financially if your business failed?

(a) Yes with a bit of cutting back (10)

(b) No (5)

(c) You don't know (0)

3 What will you do with your children while you work?

(a) I will work around them (5)

(b) I'll find a relative to look after them (0)

(c) I have childcare sorted (10)

4 Why do you want to do this?

(a) You're bored (0)

(b) You see this as a viable way to make money (10)

(c) You need a change (5)

Add up the scores that appear in brackets after the answers you have chosen and see what they reveal below:

Results

0–10

You need to discuss your plans with your family, not only to keep them in the loop but also because you will need their help and input if you plan to work from home. Financial aspects have also to be considered, as most businesses don't pay out a large wage in the first year (although there are exceptions), so you need to work out how your family finances will be affected, how you will pay for childcare and where you will find the funding for your business. Starting up just because you're bored or fed up is a reason, but not the best basis for a business venture.

15–25

Your family may know what you're up to but you may not have the back-up and support you need. When planning a business don't assume that things will take care of themselves. Sweat the small stuff and look at the details. If you think you'll work round your children, first chart your average day and see how much real time and concentrated time you have to play with. You may believe in your idea, but how will you manage financially if it fails? Finally, although a change is as good as a rest, it isn't the best reasoning behind setting up alone from home.

30–40

You've laid the foundations for your business in that you have family support and have worked out the financial impact it will have. You know you're looking at a huge change of lifestyle that won't just affect your role at home but also your partner and your family. Forfeit is the name of the game here: in order to work from home you'll have to forfeit your time with your partner, sleep, weekends and leisure time.

Your working style

1 In order to work I need:
(a) To be not bothered by anyone (0)
(b) A space of my own (10)
(c) To feel passionate about what I am doing (5)

2 I am motivated when:
(a) Someone spurs me on (0)
(b) A deadline is upon me (5)
(c) I'm allowed to drive a project forward (10)

3 What I'll miss most about the office is:
(a) Being able to work as part of a team (0)
(b) Chats round the coffee machine (5)
(c) The regular money (10)

4 I like my workday to:
(a) Start and stop at the same time every day (10)
(b) Be casual and laid-back (5)
(c) To be as short as possible (0)

Add up the scores that appear in brackets after the answers you have chosen and see what they reveal below:

Results

0–10

Think twice before starting up, as working alone and from home may not be the best idea for you. If you need someone to crack the whip, or you can't scrape yourself off the floor on a bad day and love having colleagues to see you through work projects, being a sole worker isn't for you.

15–25

You may need to change your attitude about how you work when you work alone. Whereas it is possible to carve out a calm and laid-back working environment at home, working for yourself and being a mum means being a jack of all trades who's on the go all the time. No waiting for deadline fever to get you going, and no days spent emailing and surfing the Internet. Instead, you have to balance your new business and family life in a way that allows you to use up every minute of the time you have to work in.

30–40

Your working style is suited to working on your own. You like to have a set time each day to work, a space to work in and you are aware of what you'll miss most about working for someone else. It may appear regimented to others, but when you're time-starved at home this is what allows you to get the most out of your working life.

Your skills

1 With regard to your new business, you have:
(a) All the skills you need (0)
(b) Some skills, but are willing to learn the rest (10)
(c) A variety of skills and, if needed, will look for people to fill in the gaps (5)

2 When it comes to the financial aspects of your business:
(a) You've sought (or will seek) outside help (10)
(b) You'll deal with it when you have to (5)
(c) You'll get by on what you know (0)

3 When it comes to criticism:
(a) You find it hard to take (5)
(b) You don't tolerate it (0)
(c) You listen if it's constructive (10)

4 If you don't know something you:
(a) Ask someone who knows (10)
(b) Find out for yourself (5)
(c) Blag it (0)

Add up the scores that appear in brackets after the answers you have chosen and see what they reveal below:

Results

0–10

Your skills need developing. You may have all the skills required for your current job, but running your own business is rife with challenges, which means you won't have all the skills that are needed. Believing you do is a recipe for disaster. Talk to others who have started up on their own and find out the pitfalls so that you can be prepared.

15–25

You're a great self-starter who's able to work on her own, but sometimes you can't do it all on your own. It would be worth finding a mentor who can help you to see where the potential holes in your idea and business strategy might be before you take it any further.

30–40

You're wise enough to know you can't possibly have all the skills you need to run your own business, and you're clever enough to start finding the people who can help before you start up. Utilise all the free information out there before you start, and network to find the best people to help you fill in the gaps in your knowledge.

Your business

....

1 You know your business will work because:

(a) You've brainstormed the idea with others (5)

(b) You've tested it on a small market (10)

(c) You have a gut feeling (0)

2 You want to start this business because:

(a) You feel passionate about it (5)

(b) You know it will work and make money (10)

(c) You're looking for excitement (0)

3 Your idea is:

(a) Good, and you know it works (5)

(b) Unique, but you're not sure what to do next (0)

(c) Viable, because you've worked out the figures (10)

4 Your unique selling point (USP) is:

(a) You're the kind of person who would buy your product/service (10)

(b) Your work background (5)

(c) You have no idea (0)

Add up the scores that appear in brackets after the answers you have chosen and see what they reveal overleaf:

Results

0–10

When you start a business you need to be very clear about your USP, and why your potential market would come to you in preference to your competitors. If you don't know what makes you and your product or service stand out from the crowd, you won't be able to utilise your opportunities and so won't be able to make your business a success. The primary starting block is to research your idea so that you can see if your business actually has legs or not.

15–25

Your business idea is in its early stages and what you have to do now is test out your potential market to see if your idea works. Once you can see that it does, the next step is to work out if you can make a profit from it. You might be in it for creative and passionate reasons, but if you can't make a living from your business, it's pointless to start it up.

30–40

You've taken a practical approach to your business, which means it has a chance of succeeding. You know your market, how much money you might be able to make and what makes you stand out from the crowd.

Are you a Kitchen Table Tycoon?

Now add up the scores for all the quizzes to get a total score and see whether you are a Kitchen Table Tycoon:

0–45

Being a Kitchen Table Tycoon may not be right for you. Although you like the idea of setting up from home, the reality is more trying than you think. Write a pros and cons list considering everything – from what you'll miss at work to what you'll gain from being at home – and see whether it's really for you or not.

50–100

Taking into account your scores above you should be able to work out which areas need more work to help you become a Kitchen Table Tycoon. Although there's no better feeling than running your own business, make sure you are prepared for the ups and downs of business life. A good idea is one thing – a good business is another.

105–160

Potentially, you have it in you to be a Kitchen Table Tycoon: you know where to start when it comes to selling yourself, you have your family's support behind you, and you know what areas you need to seek help in.

Can you handle working from home and for yourself?

....

'You need to be self-motivated – a quiet house, empty bed and a good book can look very appealing, but you need to use your work time to work!'
Melissa Talago, Peekaboo Communications

Over the years of working from home, many people have said to me, 'You're so lucky' and in some ways I can see their point: I have no commute, no set work day, no office politics, and I don't have to work out what I am going to wear every day. Plus, for me the biggest 'lucky' part of all is that I don't have to put my daughter into full-time nursery. On the other hand, when some people say those words to me, I know they are imagining that I spend my days waking up when I want to, dipping into daytime TV when I'm bored, going for coffees with friends and generally using my days at home as they would at weekends.

The reality is hugely different. Whereas working from home is fantastic, because you get to be in your own space, choose what you do each day, and be on hand to look after your kids, the list of what I don't like is as follows:

➤ Work interrupts home life, and vice versa.

➤ Working from home is distracting – if domestic duties don't get to you, childcare ones will.

➤ It's hard to stay in work mode when you can hear your child crying/screaming/breaking something, even though someone else is looking after them.

➤ It's hard to switch off at the end of the day.

➤ When something goes wrong with your phone line/
wireless connection/post you feel totally helpless.

➤ You have to do all the administration yourself.

➤ Sink or swim, it's down to you.

➤ It can feel isolating and lonely, especially when you're
having a bad workday.

All this means that if you're considering setting up your
fabulous new business from home you need to work out
your possible pros and cons of a life at home working alone
to see if you can really cope with it – bearing in mind that,
like any big change, it takes time to get used to it. You really
need to give yourself six to twelve months to get used to
working alone, but also to get used to being by yourself,
and working from your kitchen table. So, to help you make
your decision, here are a few pros and a couple of big cons of
working from home.

YOU'RE IN CHARGE

Possible reasons to start a business from home include the
fact that you get to be the master of your own universe.
Which means if you're sick of office politics, being bossed
about, and having to do the work you hate, working for
yourself means the only person you'll ever have to answer
to is yourself! You call the shots, the hours you work and
the projects you take on as well as how you map out your

workday. The scary part is, of course, that all decisions – both good and bad – are down to you. However, if you're looking for autonomy, a chance to be motivated by what you do, a chance to be creative and independent as well as to achieve a better work–life balance, working from home is for you.

YOUR KIDS

Perhaps the most important plus you'll get from working from home is that you'll get to see more of your kids. This can be a dual benefit because if your kids currently spend most of their day at nursery or a childminder's or being cared for by relatives, working from home will give them the benefit of seeing you more throughout the day and having you parent them and play with them more often. Better still, it will also reduce the need for expensive full-time childcare.

YOUR WORKING HOURS AND COSTS

Be aware that if your aim is to work when your kids are asleep or even to work as your kids play around your feet – think again. Working from home means just that, working in your home, which means that you still need to sort out some sort of childcare, as you won't be able to run a business with very young kids or babies around you. This means you need to choose your working hours very carefully. Whereas there will be no more getting up at the crack of dawn to commute, then having to join the scrum to get home, you still need to be able to work around your kids' needs; for example, this means working in short spurts when they are at nursery, school or with a sitter, and probably outside of regular office hours. While this doesn't necessarily mean you'll work fewer hours, it does mean you'll be able to balance family and home life more easily.

Best of all you'll have lower overheads, as you'll have no fancy office space to hire, no full-time nursery fees, no commuting costs (not to mention all those takeaway cappuccinos and lunches), which means that aside from office equipment and childcare costs you'll save a considerable amount of money.

GOING WITH YOUR OWN IDEAS

Working for yourself means that at last you'll get to be creative, do things your way and run with your own ideas. This is a huge plus when it comes to running your own business, especially if you've been working in an area you've hated for a long time. But it also means that no matter how creative you get, you have to be clear about your concept, clear about your aims and focused about your market (see Chapters 2, 3 and 4 for more on this).

IT'S A REAL JOB

Don't be fooled into thinking that working from home and for yourself is not like a proper career. Take a look through some of the Kitchen Table Tycoon Profiles in this book and you'll see that there is big money to be made in running your own business, as long as you are willing to get through the start-up process, work on your idea and run your business like a business.

Just a small aside, though: don't opt to start your own business from home if you think it means working fewer hours, earning more money and suffering zero mummy guilt. Unless you have other financial means, running a business from home and working alone means no closure at the end of the day, and working just as hard as you would for someone else (if not harder). The only difference is you'll be able to mix and match your hours and so be able to do kid-friendly things when you need to, such as picking up your kids from school, taking the afternoon off to see their school play or taking a day off when they're sick. Plus, initially, your company may well eat money; meaning, you might not get a wage for a year, and you'll have to make sacrifices everywhere – as well as deal with the uncertainty of when the next bit of money will come in.

YOU'LL STILL FEEL GUILTY

Finally, it's worth bearing in mind that nothing ends your guilt when you're a mum. Although it might be at its most intense when you're miles away from your kids, sitting in an office, it will still exist when you're working from home. In fact it will be harder to ignore and deal with when you're trying to get some work done and you can hear your kids screaming for you in another room, even though you have someone caring for them, or simply hearing them having fun with someone else.

GETTING REAL

Now that you've spent some time working out if you're suited to working alone, and from home, your next step is to make sure that what you are planning to do for a living is (a) something you believe in; (b) in sync with what you want from life; and (c) something that you have the ability to do. This means that you need to get real and ask yourself: what do you want from your home business and what can you offer it?

'I will always remember when I initially set up my first business with my husband John. I was telling a client how great John was at presenting and coming up with ideas and how I felt that he was our drive. But my client soon put me in my place and told me that he joined the agency because of me and because of my passion and drive, and that I should get out there and believe in myself. That really shook me up and I realised it was true – I had to believe in myself if I was going to make my business work.'

Rachael Talpin, AboutMyArea and Mums In Control

If it is excitement you're looking for, you'll definitely get buckets of this along with adrenalin rushes, feelings of panic, exhilarating highs and frightening lows. Running your own business encompasses all of this and what you have to learn is not to run the opposite way when something scary or frightening occurs.

If it's more money you're after, firstly you have to realise that most new companies don't make a profit in the first year, which means you won't be able to have a high salary, a company car and a PA at your beck and call. However, how successful your business becomes is down to you and your business plan, so there is no reason not to set yourself a top figure in your head that you want to aim for in the long run, and a more realistic figure for your immediate future. If you're hoping for more time off, remind yourself that whereas working from home will allow you to juggle your time more efficiently it will be at the cost of your social life; meaning, more time spent with the kids during the day means more time spent working at night and at weekends when your husband is at home. Also, bear in mind that you'll be at the mercy of others in terms of your potential clients/market/suppliers and so on.

Finally, have you really got what it takes to be a business owner? Although it takes all types to run a business there are certain qualities that will get you further than most.

BEING A RISK TAKER

You can't play it safe all the time; you also need to have the ability to take risks; that is, take measured risks – the risks you can afford. Whereas handing in your resignation is tempting, it's a road to ruin if you haven't worked out a way to pay your household bills, and fund your new business. So, start by working out a business plan (see Chapter 4) that shows you where you're going and what you're going to do – and the excitement and fulfilment will come from what you're doing, not what you've done.

CONFIDENCE

In terms of your having a business you believe in, confidence is a major area to consider. Studies show that when it comes to self-belief many women hold themselves back, which is why it's worth reminding yourself over and over that the first rule of business is to believe in what you're doing. This means knowing your business and market inside out, so that when you're challenged about it, you can hold your head up and state your case. It's also about believing in yourself and your capabilities, because when you start out you're unlikely to know and understand everything about your business, but this isn't necessarily a handicap as long as you believe you can do it and are taking steps to educate yourself along the way.

'If you're willing to stand down at the first hurdle it's no good. Entrepreneurs don't do that. You have to believe in yourself.

Constructive criticism is fine but never let people tell you you're wrong about your idea.'
Louise Potts, Naked Body Care

COMMITMENT

You may think you're committed now but will you still be six months down the line when you've had three hours' sleep a night, haven't had a sociable night out for weeks, and can't afford to go out to get your hair cut? Commitment to your business is about all this and more, and it means that you have to be willing, when you start out, to make personal sacrifices, work long hours and lose your spare time until your business is up and running.

INITIATIVE

Part of the problem of working for others is that you get used to being told what to do and when to do it. Working for yourself is wholly different and requires you to take the initiative, whether this means taking a leap of faith with your idea, or trusting a supplier/manufacturer, or calling up an established business person and asking them for their advice or to be your mentor.

'I talked to my daughter's friends' mothers who were part-time professionals and they gave me lots of free advice. One is a business accountant/strategist and the other is a designer/stylist. In fact I've done this a lot with friends and friends of friends, and I think when you're starting up it's a resource you can't underestimate.'
Louise Millar, Memoir Publishing

DETERMINATION

The road to success can be a rocky one and it takes perseverance to pick yourself up when things go wrong and/or when
you've had a major setback; that is, you have to be prepared
for financial insecurity, risks that go wrong and people who
let you down, and then have the determination to pick yourself up and carry on.

> 'I had a number of setbacks that meant I had to rebrand and
> set about winning back my company name in court. I did
> eventually win, but the rebranding cost me and I was awarded
> limited damages. What I learned from these incidents is that
> you have to be able to bounce back over and over again and
> carry on if you want to run your own business. I had faith in my
> product, and thankfully I had the support of friends and family
> around me saying, "I believe in you" – and that's what got me
> through the challenges.'
> **Sally Preston, Babylicious**

RESILIENCE

Are you flexible, able to be the power behind your idea
and resilient enough to deal with the uncertainty and un-
familiarity of running your own business? If so, being your
own boss could turn out to be the best decision you've ever
made.

Have you got a business head?

Alongside personal traits you also need to consider your
business skills. There are four skills that every business owner

needs to ensure they have got to grips with before starting their business in order to help them (a) understand their business; and (b) make their business work. Knowing where you stand on the following skills will allow you to see where your strengths and weaknesses are and where you need to fill the gaps.

> 'Right from the beginning I had the confidence to know I could start a company, but realised that I had no marketing skills, so I employed a company and outsourced to specialists for brand design.'
> **Sally Preston, Babylicious**

1 FINANCIAL SKILLS

This is the area that scares most people, and rightly so, because if you don't understand the finance aspect of your business, you're unlikely to be able to make your business work. However, don't panic, because even if you can't balance your personal accounts, it doesn't mean that you won't be able to run a business with a little help. Firm up your skills with a business course on finances, and get an accountant. Above all educate yourself about terms such as gross profit, net profit, and cash-flow projections (see Chapter 5 for more on this) as well as credit management.

2 DEVELOPMENT SKILLS

Do you understand how you are going to make long-term plans for your product or service and how you're going to find your customers, market your product and sell it? If not, you need to assess the strengths and weaknesses of your business (and yourself) and work out ways of getting to grips with its development (see Chapter 4 and 6 for more on this) and how you'll face competition.

3 CUSTOMER SKILLS

You may be selling a product or service that you know you would buy, but how are you going to sell it to others? How will you find your customers, attract them to your product and get repeat business from them? What's more, where will you reach them and how will they find you (see Chapter 4 and 6 for more on this)?

4 MARKETING AND PR SKILLS

You could have the best business idea in the world, but if no one knows about you, or you can't identify what sets you apart from the field, or analyse your potential market and work out how to make your customers repeat business, you won't be able to make your business work. The good news is that you can learn about marketing skills and PR (see Chapter 6 for more on this) without spending a fortune, with a little bit of research and common sense.

Finally, once you have evaluated everything to do with working for yourself and from home, make the decision. Make it in your head and decide that this is absolutely what you want to do. If you're still stuck, imagine how you'll feel if you never follow through with this idea. Visualising your future is a good way to find out whether or not you're on the right path. So picture yourself five years down the line still working for someone else every day and living the life you live now. Do you feel a sense of dread, a sinking feeling of depression, or are you secretly relieved that you haven't gone for your own business?

Now swap scenarios and picture yourself working from home over the next five years – does it feel as if you have done the right thing, and are you happy with your decision? If so, you have your answer – now all you have to do is go for it!

KITCHEN TABLE TYCOON PROFILE
Sally Preston
Business: Babylicious – Sally Preston is the award-winning entrepreneur behind the frozen baby foods

'There I was one day, puréeing yet another batch of chicken casserole at midnight when I thought: this is crazy, why doesn't anyone make delicious-tasting frozen baby food that I want to buy, to save me the hassle.

I then realised that there were many other mums like me saying exactly the same thing, eager to give their kids the best food possible but without the time to do it. So, using my skills as a food scientist with 11 years' experience in ready-meals for Marks & Spencer, and combined with being a mum with a consumer need, I started Babylicious and Kiddylicious frozen meals.

Right from the beginning I had the confidence to know I could start a company, but realised that I had no marketing skills, so I employed a company and outsourced to special-ists for brand design. Everything else was planned from my dining-room table. I never made the food there but it was from home that I found a factory to make the food legally and safely, planned the recipes, bought the raw ingredients, sold to retailers and did all the invoicing. Like many people starting up I started off doing everything for myself, which means there's no role in this company that to this day I've not done, which I feel is important.

My vision from the start was a national brand, not a cottage industry, so I visited all the high-street banks for funding and wrote a business plan. All the banks thought it was a great idea and offered me money, but they also thought it was too obvious an idea, and felt that there had to be risk associated with it, so although they'd lend me money, all put high penalties and interest on the loan, so I had to walk away. In the end I remortgaged my house and borrowed from my parents. I then thought up the name with friends and registered it as a trademark right away.

However, in the three-week gap between registering the company and incorporating the name, someone deliberately and maliciously took the name. This setback meant I had to rebrand and set about winning back the name in court. I did eventually win but the rebranding cost me and I was awarded only limited damages. If that wasn't enough, I was then the victim of a hoax caller who told all my customers I was under investigation by the Advertising Standards Authority. What I learned from these incidences is that you have to be able to bounce back over and over again and carry on if you want to run your own business. I had faith in my product, I knew mothers loved it and, thankfully, I had the support of friends and family around me saying, 'I believe in you' – and that's what got me through the challenges.

My advice to anyone starting up is simply to do all your homework and persevere. Know your product and give people a reason to meet with you. It's not easy but you can do it. The best bits of owning my own company are simply that I'm in control of my life – meaning I can go to my kids' sports days and assemblies and I can come and go as I please. The feedback from mums also gives me a lift and a buzz and, above all, I love it that, although my children come first, my working life is great fun.'

KITCHEN TABLE TYCOON PROFILE

Louise Millar

Business: Memoir Publishing – a publishing company that produces private memoirs for individuals

'After my father died I became aware of how much family history had gone with him and I wished we had recorded it. A year later, a friend, who knew I was a journalist, told me her mother wanted to pay someone to write her biography and so I decided to research this as a business idea.

At first I felt uncomfortable about starting such a large venture on my own so I asked an experienced journalist friend to be my partner. His help was invaluable at the start, as we brainstormed everything from market research to cover designs. However, he decided it was too much of a risk for him to leave his well-paid job. I was concerned about going it alone, but then I decided to go for it and found I enjoyed the freedom of making decisions by myself.

I started by writing my friend's mother's biography for free to create a sample. From this I calculated the costs and time involved – and worked out whether I would enjoy the reality of writing and producing memoirs as a job. I employed a designer to create a design template for the books and covers, and another friend, an intellectual property lawyer, to advise me about all the legal issues – important in publishing – and I funded it all with credit cards and a loan from my family.

Early on I realised that I couldn't afford professional market research so I spent a lot of time talking to people of my generation and my parents' generation, and identified two main client groups: high-income adults who would like their parents to write a memoir, and retired people who wanted to do it for their children. Personal contacts in the City suggested word-of-mouth – or viral – advertising works best there, so samples are currently circulating in the City via personal contacts there. I also risked a considerable part of my start-up budget on a large advertisement in a magazine aimed at this age group two weeks before leaving my permanent job.

Then, before leaving my job, I took the opportunity to discuss what I was doing with some high-level female editors there, to get the benefit of their experience. They advised me that I was under-pricing my product, apparently a common mistake that women make in business. They also advised me to stop paying for expensive classified ads and to use my extensive contacts in magazines, and theirs, and to write a press release and send it out as soon as possible for free publicity. My advertisement in the magazine proved them right on that point. However, I managed to get some free editorial and have not advertised since, by approaching a local north London glossy arts magazine that wrote features on local businesses. I also wrote a piece for them that was picked up by the *Observer*, who paid me to do an article for them and this in turn was picked up by the *Irish Times* and Irish radio and led to six new commissions – and all at no extra cost to me.

My objectives for the first year were to receive commissions for 12 memoirs, expand my advertising/PR and pay off all the start-up costs. I also wanted the products to be of very high quality to get the best possible word-of-mouth recommendations, because there are other businesses doing the same thing, so I knew I needed to use my unique experience as a former senior editor of a national magazine as a selling point.

The highs have been: the first phone calls coming in after I advertised; the freedom of my first Monday morning working at home; the enjoyment of doing this job and seeing all my hard work benefiting me and my business rather than someone else's business; my friend telling me that she had cried when she read her mother's memoir; and when the first book arrived looking like a "proper book".

The lows have been: sleepless nights wondering if I was mad to give up my job; a major disaster the month my advert appeared in the back of a magazine and finding that all my competitors were listed for free in editorial at the front alongside a feature on how to write your own memoir; discovering legal loopholes that nearly scuppered the business before launching; having a major miscommunication with my designer because I had, due to our friendship, been too casual and not put my instructions in writing; finding out that it appeared impossible to get a grant to start a business; getting phone calls in response to my advert but not being ready with a website or even headed paper due to a limited budget.

Also, I have been so keen to find customers that I didn't price the product correctly. I didn't charge for travel costs, and also ended up paying extra at the printing stage to get the book to look better, which I should have really passed on in the price. This made me toughen up and begin to charge properly. I've also realised it's important to keep evolving, so I am adding to the website, finding new products and redesigning old ones.

My advice to anyone considering working for themselves is not to do it until you have an idea that is so perfect for you that it just seems to have a momentum of its own. Right from the start I realised that my idea would fit all my former work experience – as a production journalist, a commissioning editor and an experienced real-life story writer – and I just felt incredibly confident and optimistic about it, to the point where I was worried that I wasn't worried. It helped my confidence that everyone, from my lawyer to my neighbours, generally agreed that it was a very good idea.

My plans for the future are: to expand the business so that it grows from 12 commissions a year to 100 a year, most of which will be freelanced out to other writers. I am also developing a cheaper DIY memoir package to sell to the many customers who have been interested but unable to afford the cost of the journalist-written memoirs. Now that all the start-up costs have been paid off after the first year, I can introduce this at hardly any extra cost. Hopefully, I can eventually employ a business manager to help me expand so that I can concentrate on the creative side of the business.'

KITCHEN TABLE TYCOON PROFILE

Melissa Roske

Business: Wheels in Motion Coaching – life coaching

'I've always worked from home as a journalist, but after my daughter started school I wanted to expand my horizons, and started to read about coaching, which seemed a natural progression for me. I knew that if I wanted to be a life coach, I'd better get the proper training and credentials needed to qualify as a certified coach. So I enrolled in New York University's coaching certification programme. I also began coaching my very first clients, and racking up the hours needed to get certified by the International Coach Federation (ICF).

The hardest part of setting up on my own was that I knew little, if anything, about starting up a viable business. Therefore, I had to figure out how to establish a Web presence, how to market my coaching services (and to the right audience), and how to find a good Web designer who could help me achieve my goal. It was quite daunting. The thing is, although coaches love nothing more than to coach, more than 50 per cent of our time is devoted to marketing our services. The catch-22 is that, not surprisingly, most coaches know precious little about marketing and are thus unable to generate and sustain much business. As a result, many new coaches end up quitting the profession out of frustration and lack of motivation.

One of the problems I faced was that I wasn't clear about who my target audience was. For instance, I currently focus on coaching women – "Women with a Drive for More!" – exclusively, but I do need to narrow my focus further to attract more clients.

However, running my coaching business from home means that, in addition to being able to coach in my PJs and bunny slippers (!), I'm able to be more flexible than if I were working out of an office. This flexibility also allows me to pick up my daughter from school, to shuttle her to and from her after-school activities, and to host play dates. Working from home also means that I am more accessible, and that I get to spend more time with my family – particularly my daughter. I'd say it's a win-win situation.

My tips to other mums who want to give it a try are:

• If a self-run business is something you want and need in your life, then by all means throw caution to the wind and go for it. Trying something new on for size, and perhaps even failing at it, feels a lot better than sitting around wondering, "What if …?" or "Why didn't I …?"

• Of course, this sort of relaxed, devil-may-care attitude is easier when you have a safety net to cushion your fall (ie, a supportive partner who's ready and able to pay the bills). But still, doing something you love, are serious about and truly committed to have got to be worth the risk. And if you fail? At least you can say, "I gave it my best shot." You can't fault a person for trying, right?

Perseverance, stick-to-itiveness, extreme optimism, creativity, and a tough skin are all qualities that are worth having if you're going to go it alone!'

KITCHEN TABLE TYCOON PROFILE

Rachael Talpin

Business: AboutMyArea now has 240 franchisees across the UK and is worth £2 million pounds. Mums In Control is Rachael's new business and helps mums find work they can fit round their children

'I've been in business now for 12 years, as I originally started an advertising agency in May 2005 with my husband John called JRT Advertising. Funnily enough it was actually John that always wanted to be his own boss, I had a great job and was very successful as a sales manager at a radio station in Birmingham, BRMB, and I don't think I would have set up in business if it wasn't for him.

We ran the company for eight years and in the last year won a massive £10 million account, but just as we invested in our company to meet the needs from that account, the company cut their spending and wouldn't compensate us for what we'd spent and we ended up losing the business. It was a tough time because we had to remortgage, sell our car, cash in our pensions and take out a loan to clear our debts.

While we were thinking about what to do I created a local magazine that went back to basics advertising local businesses. It was such a simple idea but it encompassed everything I believe in – community spirit and small busi-nesses. In the first month I made £3,000 from a few hours work. So I decided to create a website based on the same idea, knowing nothing about the Internet. Luckily I found an excellent designer who worked on a profit-share basis and I haven't looked back.

After just six months we managed to pay off the last of the loans we'd taken out and AboutMyArea is now worth £2 million and has 240 franchises. Better still it's enabled me to work from home and spend more time with my daughter. In many ways because we were broke when I started up it was the scariest and most stressful time of my life, but also the most rewarding as it made me realise what I had missed in the past by putting my work above my family.

In fact it was this that inspired me to set up my next business www.mumsincontrol.com – a website to help mums find work that fits round their children. In fact all of my business ideas have come through experience and a feeling that I wish I had that service or business offered to me. I truly believe you have to have passion and belief in a product or service so actually makes your business.

Mums In Control was put together knowing that as a first-time mum myself there wasn't much support out there for women who wanted to work flexibly for themselves around their children, so I thought it would be great if we could all pull together and inspire other mums to believe in themselves and create an opportunity for themselves.

If I were to do it all over again, I'd probably do everything differently, you learn so much when you work for yourself, and make so many mistakes, but that makes you who you are today. My steepest learning curve has been to learn how to stop worrying and let things go. When you are in business you have the responsibility of everything and everyone, and I am a real worrier and that's not a good combination. I am slowly learning to let go and realise that I can't worry about everything, I have to trust that I can only do my best in each and every given day, and I have to learn to trust the people I employ to take care of things.

My tips to women starting up are to believe in yourself, do your research and go for it, and also ask for help along the way as there's lots out there. Also be strict with yourself. I chose to work from home to spend more time with my daughter so I have to remind myself to stop work now and then and be with her and enjoy her, as well as work. As for mummy guilt, it's always there, so you have to learn to stop beating yourself up and accept the reason you are working is to provide a good life for your kids, and that means sometimes you have to compromise.

Personally I love working from home. It means I can see my daughter whenever I want, keep on top of the house and enjoy my life, but if you're going to do it don't procrastinate – working mums can't afford to dawdle. Lastly you have to be able to pick yourself up from setbacks. I went on a TV programme called *Dragons' Den* to find funding for www.aboutmyarea.com and they just ripped my business idea apart, which was very upsetting but you just have to put things like that behind you and realise it's nothing personal. Everyone in business gets knock-backs, so just tell yourself tomorrow is another day. If it's very bad look at your business plan again and re-inspire yourself. I'm proof that you can make a lovely life for yourself through sheer hard work.

Tips:

• Make sure you have your own designated area at home to work from so you can be organised.

• Get your kids to respect you're working from home. Tell them mummy needs to take a call and they can't interrupt, and then give them a reward if they respect that.

• Have a structure to your day. I start in the morning, work till 12, stop for lunch and then start again.

• Don't procrastinate – working mums don't have time to dawdle.

• Be controlled about emails – they can be very distracting.

• Don't be frightened about getting into your work. Be aware if you're using avoidance tactics.

CHAPTER TWO
The big idea

Somewhere between dreaming of running your own business and actually starting it comes the part where you have to find, consider and evaluate a business idea. For many, this is the fun fantasy part where you conjure up a multitude of possibilities and run through them in your head, but for others it's the nightmare stage, where behind every seemingly good possibility is a dead end, or simply no idea at all. The good news is that wherever you are in the idea stage – that is, you have a great one or don't have one at all – this chapter can help you to come up with an idea, define its potential as a business and work out whether or not that idea is viable.

> 'Lots of mothers are keen to start up a work-at-home business but don't know what to do. If that's you, look at what you enjoy and what you're good at – list everything. Once you've identified those things, look at the market around you and see if you can spot any gaps that you could plug.'
> **Melissa Talago, Peekaboo Communications**

The simple fact is that no matter how much you want to go into business for yourself not everyone is a creative-ideas person who can rattle off a list of ideas, spin them and work out their viability. You only have to listen to other people's business ideas to realise that most people can't work out what makes a good idea and what doesn't. However, this doesn't mean that you should give up before you even start. The process of finding ideas is one that anyone can learn to be good at, rather than it being something innate (although ideas people would swear the opposite). What you have to do is learn to think like an ideas person and search out ideas the way they do.

This means doing a number of things. Firstly, working out who you are, and what you find enjoyable in life. This may seem obvious but when was the last time you looked at your values, considered what you take pleasure in, and thought about what kind of consumer you are? (A valuable insight if you're starting your own business.) Secondly, if you want to find new ideas, you need to look beyond the obvious and expand your horizons. This means exploring every avenue open to you, as well as new ones that you may never have thought about. Dig deeper than you usually would and try to make associations between news stories or events you've heard about, information you've picked up from various media, and anecdotes from friends and family. For example, the idea for this book came from reading about the Kitchen Table Tycoon study in UK and US newspapers, having the new mums in my antenatal group ask me lots of questions about working for myself, and starting a new phase in my life as a mum who works from home.

So, consider what's on your mind right now, the problems you're coming across in your daily life, the stories you're hearing and the subjects that are triggering your imagination. Thirdly, research your ideas as they come to you. You may think that you've found a unique business proposition that everyone will need (or want) but are you sure it really is unique, and if it's so great, are you positive someone's not doing it already, and if they're not, why aren't they?

This means that whatever you come up with you have to do some market research among your friends and colleagues, as well as surfing the Internet. Investigate, examine and probe your idea until you've exhausted every option open to you, and more. Then, and only then, will you know for sure whether your idea is a possible business venture or not, and whether it's worth staking everything you have on it.

8 PLACES TO FIND A NEW IDEA:

1. In your current skill base

2. In your social circle

3. Within a life change

4. Through a mum problem

5. On the Internet

6. By meeting new people

7. In the daily newspapers

8. By investigating your local area

Finding your idea

To find a business idea consider the following five questions while letting go of your inner critic for a moment and going with the flow, then see what you can come up with. The aim is to think of a list of areas, ideas and potential ventures that suit you and your life, so that you can investigate their possibility as a business.

1 WHAT DO YOU FEEL PASSIONATE ABOUT?

What do you have endless energy, passion and enthusiasm for? Your family, your children, green issues, music, eating, magazines, clothes, sport, hosting events? The list, if you really think about it, is endless, which means that whether you realise it or not, you already have a variety of rich sources to pull business ideas from.

Turning a personal pleasure or something you feel strongly about into a business is the ideal way to create one for yourself, because it not only gives you instant gratification but you're also guaranteed to enjoy what you're doing every single day. If you think you can't turn your pleasure into a viable business, try to think laterally like the following entrepreneurs did:

eBay was created after the girlfriend of Pierre Omidyar (the creator of eBay) complained to him about how difficult it was to find someone who could share the same passion and interest in her hobby on the Internet. As a result Pierre opened a small online auction store on his personal website so that Pamela could contact other collectors and also buy and sell products, and this was the start of eBay.

Sahar Hashemi, a former lawyer, was inspired to set up a chain of coffee bars in the UK (known as Coffee Republic) after she found herself spending a large amount of time in coffee bars in New York when visiting her brother.

Janine Allis set up a juice bar in Australia when she realised that even though she was into healthy living there weren't any healthy fast-food options for her to offer her kids.

Here are some suggestions to get you started:

➤ If you feel passionate about green issues, your kids, and health issues, you could run an ethical clothing company. You could start a range of products aimed at a certain group such as environmentally friendly toiletries, or come up with some sort of service that promotes your aims and beliefs (such as Boost Juice Bars).

➤ If you feel passionate about parenting, and/or your local area, you could start a community project, or run a service for new parents or kids.

2 WHAT ARE YOUR STRENGTHS?

What do you do so well that people comment on it or suggest you could make a living out of it? A good way to find this out is to ask friends, family and current or past work colleagues what it is they think you're good at. Friends often told me I should give advice for a living (a positive way of saying I was bossy). Although I couldn't see a business in this, knowing that counsellors and psychologists actually don't give advice, I became a writer on a magazine and eventually an advice columnist.

Feeling stuck about your strengths? Well, according to psychologists there are six types of intelligence, and although we all have elements of each type, each of us tend to lean more towards one of them, and this can help to point you in the right direction.

1 Intrapersonal

This means you have a strong understanding of yourself, of knowing who you are, what you can do, what you want to do and how you react to things. You could use this to become a counsellor, a life coach, or run a teaching business – or become part of a service industry.

2 Linguistic

This means you are good at verbal communication. This is great for working as a PR business, or in advertising, journalism and copywriting.

3 Visual – spatial

Your strengths lie in what you can see. This is good for design, construction, architecture and planning.

4 Interpersonal

This means you are people-smart. You understand other people, which means you are good at giving information to others, so you could do some sort of training, teaching or selling.

5 Physical – coordination and dexterity

This is good for work directly with people, so fitness work, construction and sports are possible areas.

6 Mathematical
Your power lies in logic. So, this is good for finance, research and computing.

3 WHAT ARE YOUR INTERESTS?
What are your hobbies? If you no longer have any, think back to when you were a kid. What did you love to do, what made you happy and what excited you? Did you prefer being outside to inside the house? Were you someone who liked to draw alone, or get out on your bike with friends? These may seem ridiculous questions but many a hobby has been turned into a successful business venture. For example, if you like being outside all the time or gardening, think conservation, horticulture or garden design (see Karen Lumb and Alleyn Park Garden Centre page 74).

A friend of mine's main interest lay in making cakes. Originally she worked as a PA, but her cakes were so yummy and gorgeous to look at that friends started ordering them for birthdays and baby showers, and she became overrun with orders. So she then began making huge batches at home and selling them in a local market, and thanks to the success of that she now runs her own successful bakery and café. For another friend, running and football have always been her strengths and pleasures, but as she knew she could never take them to a professional level she became an accountant, then realised she loathed it and set himself up as a personal trainer.

Here are some suggestions:

➤ If your interests are in new technology and the Internet (meaning you spend much of your day surfing the

Internet), don't underestimate what you know. You could design websites, create your own website (offering an insight into new technology for technophobes), or even take a course and set up your home business online.

➤ If your interests are shopping, buying and/or fashion, you could set yourself up as a personal shopper, or offer a gift service with a specific angle, such as buying for a new baby.

➤ If your interests lie in what you previously did for a living, then consider becoming a coach. For example, if you were an accountant you could become a financial coach or financial adviser. If you worked in human resources or a large company, consider becoming an executive coach. If personal and emotional areas are more your thing, consider life coaching. The key here is not to become one of many, but to hone your interests and what you do best into an angle for your business.

4 WHAT GAPS IN THE MARKET CAN YOU SEE?

Problem solving is an area that's rich in business ideas because, as a mum, you're likely to have already come across a multitude of 'mum problems' that don't seem to have a solution. If you can think of a solution, don't be fooled into believing your idea is too obvious and therefore must already be out there. When Sally Preston (Babylicious) came up with the idea of ready-made frozen baby-food purées for busy mums, she couldn't believe it hadn't already been done. Even the banks she went to for financing couldn't believe such an obvious idea wasn't already in the market place. Likewise, the Cuddledry baby towel was devised by two friends to combat the problem of having to lift a baby out of the bath while holding on to a towel. Unlike normal towels, the Cuddledry attaches like an apron, leaving hands free to lift a baby out of the bath, thereby ending the bath-time juggling act.

If you've spotted a similar gap in the market and have an idea to solve a baby/mum problem, your next step is to do some market research among your target group (the customers you'll potentially sell to). This will help you to find out if your idea is already out there, which is possible, and if your idea is actually what people want and need.

5 BRAINSTORM FOR THAT LIGHT-BULB IDEA

If you haven't yet got an idea, sit down with a group of friends and family and have an ideas brainstorming session. Try to put together a group of people who are very different so that they can offer you wildly different views and perspectives, as well as ideas. The key here is to make sure everyone has a different experience of life so that the ideas they all come up with are varied and different from the ones you may have already had on your own.

If you do have an idea to play with, get together with some friends and tell them what you want to do (although first make sure you totally trust the people you're speaking to) and see what they say about it, being sure to write down everything that comes to mind, regardless of whether you like their views or not.

Also, bear in mind that when you or someone else floats an idea, what people say and what people do are two different things. For example, some people think they have to tear an idea apart when you ask for their opinion, so rather than take their word for it, use their comments to firm up your belief in your idea – if you can't do this it's possible that it is indeed a bad idea. Next, observe what your friends do. They may say they'd love organic home-made food but what do they actually buy and eat?

The aim of brainstorming is to work out what makes you excited and also to test out what's actually feasible for a kitchen-table business. For example, friends might tell you that they would definitely use a website of personally vetted boutique hotels that accommodates people with babies, but, in reality, how would you do this working from home and on a limited budget? Similarly, a business that delivers freshly made organic food may sound like a fantastic idea, but where will you cook it to comply with food regulations, and how will you deliver it?

Having said that, both ideas could work but in a different form, so what you have to do is play around with your ideas and find an appropriate angle that plays into your strengths and talents as well as your home situation. This will ensure that (a) you're not offering something you can't deliver (the kiss of death to a business); and (b) you're building a business that has a long-term potential and can actually make you money to live on.

What makes a good idea?

'When people say to me, "You're lucky", that's not true. To make a business work, it takes an inordinate amount of time and dedication. There are very few people with the tenacity

to see an idea through. If you want it, you have to make it happen.'
Amanda Tsinonis, SAReunited and Yesnomaybe

It's not always easy to say what makes a great idea, as some ideas sound ridiculous and then end up being global money-spinners, whereas others sound amazing and fall flat on their faces. However, to find out if your idea is a good one, you need to locate its USP. That's the 'unique selling point' of your business: what makes it stand out from the crowd and what makes customers come to you over everyone else. To help you find your USP think of a business you admire and write down what you feel is its USP. For example:

Coca-Cola – the real thing – as in it's the real one and only fizzy cola, a phrase that sticks in everyone's mind over all the other colas on the market, and so makes people opt for it as it's supposedly the 'original' cola.

To find your USP, talk to friends and colleagues and get their insights about your idea. Ask them what they think makes your idea stand out; why they would come to you rather than a competitor and why your product or service appeals to them. If they're on the same page as you, you're on to a winner. If, however, they're missing what you feel is your USP it's likely you have either sold your idea badly or simply overestimated the value of the idea.

To get it right try to encapsulate your business idea into a sentence, incorporating exactly the uniqueness of your business, so that people get it instantly.

To find your USP, list all of the benefits you offer to your customers. Write down everything you can think of. Is there one major benefit that stands out that other companies don't offer? If the answer is 'yes', that's your USP. If the answer is 'no', you probably don't have one, so try to create one. Try adding something to your business that you're not already doing. Put yourself in your customers' shoes. If you were being approached with this idea, what would it take to get your attention? What can you add to your business that your competitors don't offer?

Remember that the benefits of knowing your USP and ensuring that others grasp it is that it will help you to make your business successful, ensure your business plan is solid, and will help you to finance it in the long run – so don't skip this bit.

What makes a bad idea?

Bad ideas are plentiful and you don't have to search very far to find them. For example, in my local area there is a smart Internet café right next to a normal café that offers a free Internet wireless service, and opposite the library that offers computer and Internet use for less than the price the café charges an hour. Needless to say the Internet café is always empty. There is also a sports clothing shop near a gym and leisure centre, both of which contain discounted outlets for sports clothing and gym gear. Lastly, there are four expensive lingerie shops in a high street of only 30 shops and all are empty of customers.

By comparison there are plenty of businesses that could work very well on the high street. For example, a women's shoe shop in an area that's literally teeming with freelance women and new mums. Plus, in an area littered with yummy mummies, baby clothes shops, and baby groups there is no maternity clothing shop or shops offering beauty products to pregnant women. So the question you have to ask yourself with your idea is: if it's already being done to death, is it worth you doing it again? And if you think you have a new angle on an old idea, really consider if people will go for it, or will you be like the glamorous lingerie shops and trendy Internet café that are all empty?

The next area that makes for a bad business idea is if your idea is good but you have zero expertise in the market and are just winging it. For example, if your idea is to run a food business, do you have any expertise and knowledge of making food for the mass market? Or if you are someone who loves buying clothes don't know how to style others with differing tastes could you really be a personal shopper? Although many of these skills can be learned, the questions to ask yourself are (a) do you have time to learn them? and (b) what makes you think you can run this business better than the businesses already out there?

By far the worst business idea is to grab a trendy fad. Although it's hard to know what will be a passing trend and what won't be, if it's been done to death on your high street and everyone you know has heard of it – or ignored it – you can bet your bottom dollar your idea stinks. Ideas that have gone by the wayside include popcorn shops (who wants 30 different flavours of popcorn, when most people only ever eat popcorn at the cinema?). Also think of the early online fashion Internet sites, which weren't bad ideas (as they work extremely well today) but were ahead of their time when

Internet shopping was in its early days and no one really trusted shopping on the Internet.

Finally, a bad business idea is one that really compromises your integrity because it means you'll always be in conflict with it. At the end of the day we all have morals, standards and scruples when it comes to our personal lives, and these should cross over into your working life if you want to end up happily successful (rather than just successful) – which is why it always pays to stick to what you believe in no matter what you're being offered or what you're being told is a fantastic idea.

Turning your idea into a business

Now you have an idea that you think is feasible, the next critical stage is to develop it through research to help you see whether there really is a market for your product or service. If you have already spoken to friends who could be possible customers, take your idea further afield. If your target market is other mums, take it to your local new mums' class, or ask a local nursery if you can put a sign up. If you're offering a service, offer free tasters where your customers hang out and see if your idea is taken up. For example – a ten-minute massage if you're a therapist, or a taster of your cakes if you're a baker, or a free homemade card, if that's your new business. When someone contacts you, don't be afraid to ask questions to see what was tempting about your offer and what attracted them to you.

'My market research was mainly loitering outside large department stores with a clipboard and asking people if they wanted
reasonably priced chemical-free natural toiletries. I then spent
hours researching products online and reading up on the
causes on eczema, and I even phoned former colleagues for
details of beauty manufacturers, so that I could cold-call them.'
Louise Potts, Naked Body Care

To find out if there is a market, here are the key questions
you need to ask yourself:

➤ Who is your customer and can they afford what you are
offering?

➤ What is unique about your service or product?

➤ What is the best way to attract new customers?

➤ What is the best way to ensure repeat custom?

➤ Does your product or service comply with local or relevant industry regulations?

➤ Are you just banking on a passing trend? (Although this
can be hard to assess – many people thought mobile
phones, the Internet, coffee and bottled water were
passing trends originally!)

At the same time as doing the above, you need to seek out
your competition. Surf the Internet to see who is doing the
same thing as you on a local and a global level and don't be

afraid to contact them for advice. They might tell you to get lost, or they might actually be able to offer you some valuable insight and help. And don't be embarrassed to cold-call – everyone does it, as it not only helps you to see what you're up against but also whether your idea is worth doing or not. After all, if there are already ten people offering the same service or product as you, it's pointless to start another business, unless you can offer something different.

Likewise, look at the businesses that aren't working in your market. For example, if you're interested in manufacturing or selling kids' clothing, take a look at the sites and shops that don't seem to be making an impact or that simply aren't working. Try to see those businesses in the same way a customer would, and work out why you wouldn't buy from them, use them, and/or recommend them to others.

Next, be sure to time-manage yourself and build a plan that will take you from the idea stage to the start-up stage. Sort out short-term, mid-term and long-term goals. Short term should encompass a couple of weeks, and can be anything from trying competitors' products to walking the street and asking strangers what they think of your idea. Mid-term goals should be more practical things such as writing a business plan (see Chapter 4), finding financing and starting your business up. Long-term plans should be about business development, and where you expect to be in six months, a year and further down the line. Setting a time limit for all of this is vital, especially if you're a procrastinator, otherwise three months down the line you will still be at the ideas stage, afraid to take it further.

From an idea to a business

If you've tried out all of the above you'll see that there are a hundred ways to find new ideas. Below are six of the main ways to go from an idea to a Kitchen Table Tycoon – whether it's using your current skills, entering a niche market, grabbing a new trend, turning a hobby into a business or going with your gut instinct.

IDEA 1: THE CAREER SIDESTEP

Using your current skill base as a home business.

KITCHEN TABLE TYCOON PROFILE

Melissa Talago
Business: Peekaboo Communications – a communications and marketing consultancy specialising in the tums-to-tots sector

'I'd been in PR for 12 years before I set up on my own, working primarily in the technology field for Microsoft and IBM. After I had my first baby, the company I worked for wasn't into flexible working so I started freelancing. By the time I had my second baby I decided I just couldn't work in technology PR any more and needed a change.

Then one day when I was particularly sleep deprived, I decided to make baby food for a living. While researching the sector I came across the baby-food company Babylicious and couldn't believe I hadn't heard of it before. I realised that making baby food wasn't for me, but thought I could play a role in helping to promote Babylicious. I wrote to the owner, Sally Preston, saying that I thought there was more she could do to create awareness of her products among mums. She agreed to let me promote her and that's how Peekaboo Communications started.

After that I noticed how many other parents start up their own businesses selling baby-related products and services once they have children, and that most of the ideas behind these businesses are brilliant but few have the time or skills to get their companies noticed in a crowded marketplace. So, Peekaboo helps raise their visibility through cost-effective PR and marketing campaigns. As a mum, I completely understand their target audience and I understand the pressures they're under to run a small business while still spending time with their children. We quite regularly schedule calls around nap time.

Since then I haven't really advertised for clients, I simply went on parenting forums and my clients have come by word of mouth. Now I have a large variety of mumpreneur clients; mostly they are the little guys and don't have huge budgets, but it's a pleasure to work with them.

Peekaboo works for me because I wanted to work from home. I do get cabin fever occasionally, but I love my work because I have no commute, and I can work around my kids' nursery times, which means being there for them so that they can really benefit from having me around. As my website says, "I can change a nappy, type with one hand and read a pop-up book all at the same time" – juggling work and kids takes multitasking to a new level!

I think the biggest challenge for mothers who go into business for themselves is to get the balance right and to be able to switch between work and mummy mode instantaneously. It's something that's very tricky but has to be done if you want to run your business from home.

The highs for me are getting press coverage for my clients that really helps their businesses grow, but the lows are not being able to do what I want to do because I have no childcare. It's also hard to network after normal working hours, which I think is essential for business, but you can get round this by networking on specific sites.

For me, my plans are to keep my business small while my children are still young. Until they go to school, I am reluctant to take the leap and take on staff, because it would mean more input and I would have to put more systems in place, but I am getting to the point of outsourcing to other people, so the company is growing. It has enormous potential – but for now I'll take baby steps.'

IDEA 2: NICHE MARKET MOVES – THE BABY MARKET

Targeting your market as a new business.

KITCHEN TABLE TYCOON PROFILE

Justina Perry

Business: MamaBabyBliss – pampering and beauty treatments for mother and baby

'I had been in advertising and marketing for almost 15 years and loved it. However, when I had my second child, Alana, who is now two, I found it more and more difficult to balance work and the children (I have four, including two stepchildren) and I was constantly torn between work and home. The real turning point for me came when I realised that at the end of each day I was feeling too exhausted to enjoy precious times like bathtime and storytime with the little ones, or to give proper attention to the older ones.

I have always had an entrepreneurial spirit and loved the idea of running my own business – and I had an idea, which came to me after Alana's birth. At the time I was exhausted and in desperate need of some pampering, but there was nowhere that would entertain the notion of looking after mum and having a small baby around. I felt this was a real gap in the market because there is such a focus on being spoilt during the pregnancy but it's afterwards when you need and deserve a bit of TLC the most.

It was these factors that inspired me to develop a business that was dedicated to the nurturing and well-being of mothers and babies. I did some research, talked to friends and lots of other mothers, and MamaBabyBliss was born. I now provide pregnancy and postnatal pampering treatments for mums and mums-to-be as well as baby massage and baby yoga classes, so that mums and babies can come along together. I have a studio, a baby-friendly treatment room and I also visit mums in their homes.

It's been a fantastic experience so far, but my biggest learning curve has been how much there is to do. If I am not giving treatments and classes, then I am working on the business strategy or catching up on administration. My tips for mothers who want to start their own business from home is to set yourself a schedule and don't think of it as working from home, but as being at the office. That way you won't be tempted to go off and watch TV. But also set yourself an end of day, as it's all too easy to keep the computer on and check emails.

It is hard to maintain a good work–family balance, but I make sure that I work only a four-day week and insist on picking up my 11-year-old from school whenever I can. The best thing of all is that on most nights we can all sit down as a family for dinner and I can share developments about the company, as my husband and children have all been very involved with ideas and the creativity behind it.

I do feel that I have found my vocation, and although I am still learning a lot about business, after 18 months it has been financially worth it and I have plenty of clients. But I am now ready for my next step up, which is to develop and sell MamaBabyBliss mother and baby products, so watch this space.'

IDEA 3: GRAB A TREND

Spotting a new trend and running with it.

KITCHEN TABLE TYCOON PROFILE

Amanda Tsinonis

Business: SAReunited and Yesnomaybe – a site for finding old school/college friends and colleagues from South Africa, and a dating site

'In 2002 my eldest daughter had a severe allergic reaction and was diagnosed anaphylactic so I decided to give up my career to look after her full time, but the itch to work remained and I really wanted to start a business from home. Then one day while talking to a friend about Friends Reunited I realised that there was a gap in the market for a website for South Africans like me who were working abroad. The concept was already out there for other countries, but it had never been done by South Africans for South Africans, and I felt this is where the gap in the market lay.

I knew I had a strong marketing background, having worked on projects for top multinationals such as Kellogg's and Disney, but I also knew that I lacked the IT experience, so I asked my husband's cousin for help, as he had the right background. I then realised we needed a third person on the ground in South Africa and so asked my brother if he'd become involved.

We each put up money for the technical outlay and began to lay plans, but by this stage the UK-based Friends Reunited had already launched a South African site. We knew it was a gamble to go up against them, but we felt we understood the market better than anyone else, so within three months, and after a lot of work and perseverance, SAReunited went live. By the end of the first week, 10,000 people had joined the site and it has been growing by 500 a day ever since. We now have 625,728 total members registered, along with listings of 36,811 schools, universities and colleges and 31,702 cities and towns.

SAReunited works because we don't spam anyone, we don't sell database information and, above all, we believe the customer is king. Plus, the three of us regularly get together to think of new developments for the site. We look at trends in the marketplace, such as myspace.com and facebook.com, and structure our list of priorities. This is why a year ago we started another business: a dating site called Yesnomaybe. We originally linked to someone else's dating site, but were giving them 50 per cent of the revenue, so as we knew we could get our clients to migrate to dating, we built a dating site from scratch. In the first month we had 1,200 members and went live in the UK, Canada, US, Hong Kong, Australia, New Zealand and South Africa.

For me, having three small children, I felt guilty about being a working mother and missing out on my kids' formative years, so working from home on SAReunited is my compromise.

My advice if you've got a business idea is don't be afraid to tell people. Research it but then don't be afraid to share your project idea. It will help you define what you're doing. Also, understand your weak spots and surround yourself with people who know more than you in those areas so that you can learn from them and also be able to do what you're good at. (Primarily, I am an ideas person and I have to force myself to focus, because I always have so many ideas.) Never give up – it is hard at times, and there have been days when I have worked until 2.00 or 3.00 am but it's worth it.'

IDEA 4: TURNING A HOBBY INTO A BUSINESS

From a passion to a business.

KITCHEN TABLE TYCOON PROFILE
Karen Lumb
Business: Alleyn Park Garden Centre – specialists in high-quality and unusual plants

'My business grew out of a massive life change. At the age of 39 I discovered I was pregnant with my third child (my kids are now 18, 16 and 6 years old). At the time, I was working as a PA to a high-profile executive at an aeronautical company, and to say I was shocked is an understatement, but I used it as a way of looking at what I was doing and decided to change direction and spend more time with my family, so I left my job. When my baby was six months old I decided I needed something more than motherhood, so I enrolled on a garden design course, as gardening was something I had always been passionate about.

To complement this, on Saturdays while my husband was looking after the kids, I took a part-time job at a local garden centre to increase my knowledge and it was here that I met my future business partner. It just started by us talking about how we'd do things in a different way if we had our own centre, as we both wanted to create something that was inspiring for people who knew about gardens as well as for those who were just starting out.

From these daily chats we decided to start our own business and began working on it from home. After a lot of looking we eventually found a site that had been sitting empty for three and a half years. It was in a lovely area, which was just right for our market, but it was in a shocking state, as it used to be a builder's yard, but we took it on. It took us ten long stressful months to get it ready and it was hard work.

We were running the business from our homes, and also on site every day, painting and building walls. We even roped in all our teenage children to help. On top of this, every moment after dark I was back home on the computer making sure everything was ready for the opening, which finally happened in December 2004.

It was a fabulous feeling when we finally opened and I don't regret a thing, but my tips to anyone planning on starting a new business from home are to make sure that (a) you've got good back-up from experts such as solicitors and accountants (we didn't have that in the beginning and it caused endless grief. It's boring behind-the-scenes stuff but it's essential); and (b) listen to advice from people who have done it before (it's good to believe in yourself but don't be cocky and disregard what others in your field know, because their help is invaluable).

Alleyn Park is now exactly what I always dreamed it would be, and after just three years in business we have plans to expand and do it all again somewhere new.'

IDEA 5: GO WITH YOUR GUT INSTINCT

Do something because you feel there's a large gap in the market.

KITCHEN TABLE TYCOON PROFILE

Louise Potts

Business: Naked Body Care – an ethical range of high-quality natural body and haircare products

'I was always an entrepreneur. Even as a kid I was always making and selling things, and then at college I had a Saturday job in a salon where I made artwork to order for customers. However, the idea behind Naked didn't come about because I wanted a business but because my eldest son had very sensitive skin. I was worried about what was aggravating it so I started to look at the labels on toiletries and was shocked at how many nasties they contained. I'd previously worked in sales and marketing for a pharmaceutical company and knew that 60 per cent of what you put onto your skin is absorbed, and foaming ingredients in particular break down the natural oil barrier of the skin. The better-formulated natural products that I did find were good but so expensive that I realised there was a gap in the market for affordable pure toiletries.

My first step was to do some market research, which was mainly loitering outside large department stores with a clipboard, and it was from this that I realised I wasn't alone in wanting reasonably priced chemical-free, natural toiletries. I then spent hours researching products online, and reading

up on the causes on eczema, and even phoned former
colleagues for details of beauty manufacturers so that I
could cold-call them. Luckily, we had just moved so we
had some equity in our home that allowed me to work for
myself, but getting people to take me seriously was tough.
Eventually, though, I found some experts who worked with
me on the Naked products and suggested ingredients, and
in the end they committed to doing business with me.

All in all it took me nine months to put together a proper
proposition and a brand name, and as soon as I had my
name I trademarked it to protect it. I then also made people
at companies sign a confidentiality agreement before I
presented the idea. I do trust everyone I meet, but it's business so you just never know. When I first pitched to Boots,
my knees were knocking, but they loved the idea and said
they'd take it and put it in 600 stores. That was really scary
because it meant I took on a lot very fast and it was a huge
project to undertake and a huge learning curve for me.

As for working from home, in the beginning it was very
lonely, but the good side was I got to see my kids, and if
they were sick I was there. Even now I love it because I
don't want not to see my kids all day. Also, I am someone
who is very happy with my own company and I like to do
everything for myself, so when I was initially setting up,
being at home was a good thing, as I could focus and get
my head together. I think this is essential because you really
have to believe in yourself and your idea in order to make
it work. However, believing in yourself is a balancing act
because even though you shouldn't let other people deter

you, you have to learn to listen as well as being willing to stand your ground.

Some experts will question you from their perspective. For instance Anita Roddick was one of my business mentors and she didn't like girlie language so questioned the tone of my sales pitch, but I knew it worked, and despite us disagreeing over that, she went on to give me some really insightful advice and direction.

The highs for me are definitely my customers. I feel buoyant when they tell me that I have helped change their lives, and their letters and emails make me realise that there are real people out there buying Naked.

Alongside this I can run the company the way I want. For me the personal and ethical values in my company are very strong because Naked wasn't set up from a financial view-point. A large amount of our profits go to charities, which is very important to me, as being a mother I worry about the state of the world we're leaving for our children.

My tip, if you're thinking of doing it yourself, is don't be deterred. When I started I didn't know anything about chemicals and formulations but I made myself an expert. I called up experts in various fields and drained them of information. So, never feel embarrassed about doing this, or incapable because you feel your questions may sound stupid. Also, you have to be quite tough, as you'll be open to large amounts of criticism. It can be hurtful but you can't please everyone all of the time, so you need to have sheer grit.

Finally, make sure your family are behind you. My husband

is incredibly supportive, and all along the way he has helped me immensely by being a sounding board or helping to look after the kids. But because he is so supportive I often have to remind myself that it's time to switch off, because as much as I love my business and all that I've achieved with it, it's a toiletry brand – and for me, family comes first.'

IDEA 6: CREATE SOMETHING NEW

Invent/create/design a new product.

KITCHEN TABLE TYCOON PROFILE

Helen Wooldridge and Polly Marsh

**Business: Cuddledry Ltd – the organic Cuddledry®
baby bath towel is their first product**

'The idea for the Cuddledry towel came after a birthday party, when my friend Polly and I had all our kids in the bath. We started having a discussion about how difficult it is to pick your baby/child out of the bath when they're slippery, while holding a towel and trying to wrap them in it. We thought there must be an easier way to do it, so after they'd gone to bed we started playing around with the idea. A while later and following some market research, where we looked in depth at market trends, we got together, cut up sheets and started wrapping up teddy bears – and that's how we came up with the idea of a towel that attached to you like an apron, so that you could lift a baby up out of a bath safely.

To start with we financed the business through our day jobs and set about protecting our idea and brand, and then finding a manufacturer and a supplier. My dad is an entrepreneur so that was a help, and Polly and I are natural risk takers and doers, which also helped. However, getting involved in the nursery and gift industry has been a huge learning curve, with some real ups and downs. We received fantastic advice from others in the industry at the beginning and as a result quickly managed to get

Mothercare on board as one of our retailers.

The easiest part was that I was already freelancing in PR, and our joint skills in marketing and business development meant we understood the need for constant promotion and a clear brand. Also, I understood how to run a business from home, although this does have its limitations. Talking to a journalist or retailer from my house with my children and husband in the background isn't easy – but on the whole it works, and thanks to wireless connections I don't need a huge office set-up. As a result, I don't have a commute and my work hours are flexible, so I get to see so much more of my kids than mums in "normal" jobs.'

KITCHEN TABLE TIPS FROM HELEN WOOLDRIDGE OF CUDDLEDRY

1. Do it – just be bold and go for it. I have so many friends who say, 'You're lucky,' but I don't believe in luck, you make your own luck.

2. Get family support behind you – it's essential if you're working from home.

3. If it doesn't work, it's not the end of the world, you can start again. And it's not a failure if you do it and decide it's not for you.

4. Utilise all the support out there, so make use of the free help and find a mentor. They are really useful people.

CHAPTER THREE

Work, guilt and bad mother syndrome

'My only piece of advice to other mothers would be to think seriously about childcare and realistic available work hours. In most cases it is not feasible to turn your business off while the children are on holiday and/or during the day.'
Felicity Morgan, The Organic Flower Company

You may well be wondering why you need to read a chapter on working from home and mummy guilt when the first bit's obvious and the second bit's never going to go away. Well, if you're planning on running your own business, coming to terms with mummy guilt and working out exactly how you're going to work from home are the keys to creating solid foundations for your life. Skipping over these areas because you assume that they won't be a problem is not only a mistake but also guaranteed to place your new business on shaky ground. This is because although working for yourself has a multitude of benefits, your life isn't going to be any less rushed, frantic or stressed. In fact, if you think you were the queen of multitasking before, welcome to the Olympic arena and prepare yourself for some serious mummy–versus–work challenges.

When I first got pregnant many friends (all the ones who worked in an office, in fact) noted how lucky I was to be able to work from home, and conjured up images of me happily writing away with a cooing baby on my lap, or a sleeping baby by my side. The only lucky thing about their comments was that I knew this was a fantasy unlikely to happen. Speak to any mum who works from home and you'll find that they often feel like the CEO of both their business and family; meaning, if you're not micro-managing your family's daily pursuits, you'll be managing your business, and if you are not doing that, you'll be managing something on the domestic front – and sometimes you'll be doing all of these things, all at the same time.

Yet, 99.9 per cent of Kitchen Table Tycoons wouldn't change it for the world, because despite the fact that they have to juggle about eight thousand balls constantly, working from home does mean that they can spend more quality time with their children, as well as working on some excellent projects, making a decent living, and seeing plenty of the house that most of us are paying a fortune to live in. So, if that's your plan too, here's how to do it.

KITCHEN TABLE TIPS FROM JUSTINA PERRY OF MAMABABYBLISS

1. Be prepared for at least a 30 per cent increase in the number of grey hairs and size of under-eye bags!

2. Expect to get sick of rewriting the business plan and watching it expand day by day.

3. Realise your new best friends will be the fridge, kettle and biscuit tin.

4. Expect to experience a rollercoaster of emotions that fluctuate on a daily basis, ranging from: 'This is pants and I am going to end up a bag lady living in a cardboard box,' to 'This is really going to work!'

5. Reassure yourself on a regular basis that juggling your life is just part of the deal.

6. Realise that as a mumpreneur sometimes you'll be sitting in front of your computer emailing on a Sunday night instead of watching TV.

How to work from home

'Working from home and looking after your kids can get hectic when you become really busy. You have to discipline yourself or else you'll be on the phone to clients and putting out the washing at the same time.'
Sandra McClumpha, Fake Bake UK

Running your business from home is something many people dream of; just do a quick poll of friends and you'll find that many people like the idea of not having to commute, of rolling out of bed when they want, not having to get dressed, and simply of sitting in the garden with their laptop on their lap.

'On quiet days it can definitely be like this,' says my friend Laurie, who runs her own Web design business. 'I find myself revelling in the peace and serenity of it all. I take client calls in my PJs, answer emails from the garden and wander into my kitchen for a snack when I feel like it. Eventually, though, it ends – usually when my daughters come hurtling through the door, and suddenly my neatly piled-up files, research and invoices will be lost amidst a pile of toast crumbs, trainers and letters from school. As for my peace, well that's interrupted with shrieks, calls for help and stories from their day. It's chaotic, but it's my life.'

Parts of the above are likely to be your life, too, which is why it's essential to get some house/business rules in place, not only for your benefit but for your kids as well.

RULE 1: FIND YOUR SELF-DISCIPLINE

You may think you have self-discipline because you used to get up every day at 6.30 am and make breakfast for everyone and then get into work, but working from home demands a large and different amount of self-discipline. The problem is that whereas your home was once a place for family and relaxing, it's about to become the hub for your whole life; meaning, you're going to have to learn how to leave your kids while they are having a good time in order to work, learn how to ignore distractions such as the sofa, TV and fridge and learn to avoid doing those vital domestic tasks that have been getting on your nerves for ages.

When I first started working from home I not only had the cleanest house in the street but I also gained 4.5kg (10lb). This was because before I even got down to work each day I'd see domestic goddess duties everywhere and have to deal with them. Alongside this, every time I was stuck/bored/fed up I would fridge-surf for snacks and food. Years down the line, I have set aside a time for tidying each day, and make sure my fridge is bare of food delights; yet, I still have to exert self-discipline over cleaning everything in sight, and dealing with my daughter while my fully capable nanny or husband is around doing a great job.

Herein lies the problem of working from home: there are just too many distractions and no boss to shout, 'Stop slacking and start working!' Which means you have to make yourself be the boss and employee all at once and, every now and then, shout, 'Start working!' Other ways to maintain some self-discipline are to:

➤ View your non-work emails only once an hour (unless you're waiting for something urgent).

➤ Do all your non-work out-of-house tasks during your lunch hour as you would in an office.

➤ Set your meetings late in the day so that you're not tempted to take the rest of the day off just because it's only lunchtime and you're in town.

➤ Get dressed as if you were going to work – it will make you feel professional and, weirdly, will also make you sound professional on the phone.

RULE 2: CREATE A WORKING SPACE OF YOUR OWN

In a dream life, most Kitchen Table Tycoons would love to have a spacious office with large windows and a comfy sofa in the corner from where they could run their business. In reality, however, most hot-desk around their houses; that is, they find a space wherever they can and either work, literally, at the kitchen table, or in a bedroom or even, as one mumpreneur told me, under the stairs. However, wherever you end up you need to make sure that the space you're using is yours for the duration of your workday. This is essential if you're working from home, for a number of reasons.

Firstly, you need to feel you are in work mode, and you can't do this if you're looking at an empty juice packet, someone else's books and a pile of newspapers or dirty socks. Secondly, even if you're working from home, it's essential to feel as if you're really working and not just playing at it, and this means making whatever space you're in a clear work area. Lastly, your family needs to be able to respect that you're working, and the only way to get them to do this is for them to see that when you're surrounded by your work things you are at work. Allowing them to place their bits and pieces, and all their paraphernalia around you, will not only distract you but also allow them to feel they can get into your space whenever they want.

Ways to ensure you have a working space of your own are:

➤ To have house rules that wherever you are working is a designated work area and can't be littered with the usual house stuff until you've finished.

➤ If your children are too young to understand the above,

have an agreed sign that shows this is a work area. One friend uses a pink paperweight, another a folding screen.

➤ If your babies are crawling and pulling themselves up, make sure that wherever you work, cables, wires and laptops are not within easy reach when your back is turned for ten seconds and that you ALWAYS back up your work.

➤ Invest in five core things that you carry with you to your 'hot desk'. For me it's my laptop, diary, mobile phone, a good pen and a notebook. Wherever I am working these things are with me.

RULE 3: GET TO GRIPS WITH TECHNOLOGY

You may be a technophobe who doesn't even know how to switch on a computer, or a techno-geek who knows everything there is to know about technology (in which case you can skip this section). Or you could simply be someone who has only used computers that were previously set up for them, or used the Internet only to do their online shopping. Whatever your stance with new technology, if you're going to work from home you have to get to grips with it.

Firstly, it's going to make your life as a home business owner a hundred times easier. Back when I started (and sorry if this makes me sound like I am a 100 years old) the Internet revolution had yet to really happen, and back then faxes and answerphones were deemed to be the ultimate lifesaver. Which meant that if you didn't have one, people looked at you as if you were mad. Nowadays, whereas most people do have an email address and computer, if you are going to work from home, you have to have more than a free email account and an old computer, and you have to know more than how to switch it on.

Secondly, to look and sound professional to suppliers and customers you need to know what you're doing, not only with the Internet but also with everything from word processing to Excel sheets, even if you don't have an online business. Lastly, you have to know what to do when things go wrong, because you will have no IT department to call for help and advice.

The way to get to grips is to do a number of things:

➤ Sign up for a computer course or two – a basic one that teaches you computer skills and a more advanced one designed for people who run their business from home.

➤ Talk to mobile-phone experts who can advise you on everything from how to get the Internet on your mobile to linking in your computer to your phone, so that when you're out and about you're still accessible by email.

➤ Find yourself an IT person who can come round in an emergency – this is vital unless you know what to do when you lose your wireless connection, your service provider cuts you off or you can't download emails (if that last sentence makes no sense to you, you definitely need a basic course in online use).

➤ Keep abreast of new technology developments by talking to other business people and reading technology magazines. You never know when you'll come across something that's perfect for your business.

RULE 4: STICK TO YOUR GUNS

Also known as 'have a schedule and stick to it'. It's tempting when you first start running your business from home to get distracted by people emailing, calling and popping round. You'll usually find that all your office-based friends will call you for a chat in the afternoons when they are bored, just when you're eager for some company. However, beware: this can cut your work day in half. You have to be strong and say, 'Sorry I can't chat. I'm working.'

Likewise, you'll find that friends with kids will just drop round unannounced knowing you are guaranteed to be at home. Again, in the beginning you might find this is a great way to avoid work and have some fun, but eventually when you have to work all night to catch up you'll realise that you have to stick to your guns and make sure friends know that they can't interrupt whenever they want to. At the same time you have to make sure you don't find excuses to not work, such as baby classes and mother groups (all of which are great but not when you're supposed to be running a business).

So the rule is: if you're going to be a Kitchen Table Tycoon you have actually to work from home the way you would in an office, and just as you wouldn't allow friends to drop in to see you at work, or slink off to a morning group, you can't do it when you're working from home. Ways to ensure this are:

➤ Be clear with friends and family when you can be interrupted and when you can't during the day. And be sure you don't ruin things by breaking your own rules and calling them.

➤ Don't get addicted to email. It can be hard working alone and tempting to keep in touch, but you have to wean yourself off looking at your personal emails every ten minutes.

➤ Be strict with lunch hours. Again, when you're working for yourself, meeting a friend for a coffee or lunch can easily spiral into two hours or more.

➤ Learn to be assertive. Some people will ignore your pleas to be left alone and turn up, call or try to tempt you out. You won't want to offend them but you need to be clear about the fact that you're trying to run a business and need to be left alone to work.

RULE 5: BE ORGANISED

For an anally retentive person like myself, being organised is a pleasure. I like to have my desk tidy, my post put into one pile, and a list of daily priorities. Without this I am literally lost and can spend hours searching for something, or a whole day floundering. What being organised helps me to do is have a clear mind for work. Even if that doesn't work for you, if you're working from home it's essential to learn to be organised. Partly because this will ensure that you get things done, but also because you'll be moving your work constantly and so need to be on top of where everything is. It's also vital because your working day will be constantly interrupted so you always need to know where you are on each aspect of your job.

The main way to get organised is to sort out your child-care before everything else. It's not fair to ask your kids to 'be good' so that you can work if you intend to make a real go of your business. To work effectively you will either have to work while they are sleeping or while they are at school, and/or think about a nanny/childminder/babysitter of some sort for a certain number of days/hours a week. Although one of your aims to work from home might be to spend more time with your kids and cut down on childcare bills, you have to factor some sort of childcare into your business arrangements, or else you run the risk of either working until the early hours each day, or never truly getting your business off the ground.

Your final step is to ensure that you have a regular work schedule where you get up every day at the same time and start work (where possible) every day at the same time. You should maintain this schedule even if you're having a slack day or a bad day, because it gets you into the psyche of actually believing that you work from home. The way to do this is:

➤ Have a list of priorities each day, the top one of which you have to achieve by the end of the day.

➤ Make a clear distinction in your mind between work and non-work time, and don't drift into the wrong area at the wrong time.

➤ Tell your family when you're going to be working so they know in advance.

➤ If you are working 'overtime' make sure it's OK with family members, because whereas it's more than possible to work from your kitchen table it is also the family's kitchen table.

Mummy guilt

Guilt is the biggest thing every working mother has to contend with because once you're a mother every person has an opinion about what you should be doing, so it's probably worth accepting that you are going to feel guilt about your mothering skills and your kids until the day you die. If you believe that working from home is the ideal way to alleviate your mummy guilt you need to think again. Working while your child/children are around is just another way to feel guilty, what's more the guilt will be upfront, as your trigger will be right in front of you, probably wailing loudly for your attention.

It's worth constantly reminding yourself that you are working for your family's benefit, not to mention the fact that your children won't suffer if they have to occupy themselves for a few hours a day. What's more, new research shows that the development of children whose mothers work is on a par with kids who have stay-at-home mums; children of working mothers have similar language skills, fare just as well in intelligence tests, and develop similar relationships with their parents as the children of stay-at-home mothers.

In fact when it comes to child development what you do or don't do for a living doesn't even come into it. Researchers have found that children fare better developmentally not as a result of you being there 100 per cent of the time but through having a more stimulating home environment – with myriad books, toys and play materials – and you making a point of interacting with them by talking to them and being sensitive and responsive to their needs when you are around. It's worth knowing that mummy guilt about work is really worse for you than it is for your kids (despite their antics to make you feel bad). So here's how to keep your guilt in control, as you become a Kitchen Table Tycoon.

1 STOP COMPARING YOURSELF TO OTHERS

This is a key source of mummy guilt and one that you have to stamp out. The problem is letting yourself listen to all those non-working mums (or super-mums who somehow do it all) who go to baby singing classes, baby massage, ballet and gym classes, as well as having time to make all their own meals, is akin to stabbing yourself over and over with a sharp implement. You know you feel bad about what you can't do so why listen to people who have time to do it? Secondly, comparing your mothering skills and your children to others is an easy trap to fall into. But remember: in the same way that we don't expect to be the same as others in every other area of our life, we shouldn't expect to be the same when it comes to parenting and working. So just because some other child is super-social because his mum is a stay-at-home mum and your child is cowering behind your knees because you work, it doesn't mean you have to feel bad – your child may be shy regardless of whether you work or not. Likewise, if you know a super-successful-work-from-home mum who seems to do it all smoothly, don't let it make you feel bad. Instead ask her how she does it and garner some tips and help.

2 ACCEPT THAT YOU ARE A WORKING MOTHER

'Approach your business at the right pace and be realistic
about what you can and cannot do for your kids at this time.'
Beverley Daniels, photographer

It's no good feeling bad when you're working and feeling bad when you're with your kids. You have to accept that you work, and at times this means being away from your kids, missing something vital and having to say, 'Sorry, mummy's working.' It's tough, but by being at home your kids do have the mighty advantage of seeing you throughout the day (and vice versa) in a way that wouldn't happen if you were in an office. Make the most of this by making sure that you set times aside to see your kids. I call these moments power visits (like power naps they are short but have the clout to invigorate you) and they last around five or ten minutes and involve me having a work break to play, watch or do something kid-friendly.

You also need to accept that being a work-from-home mum will never go as planned in the same way that nothing else does when you have kids. Your children will get sick, break your laptop and scribble over a work document at a vital place. You will find yourself at a work meeting when you promised to watch them in a school play, or be so deep in concentration that you'll forget to take notice of them doing something new and amazing.

Luckily, there are ways to help you minimise these guilty feelings while struggling to become a Kitchen Table Tycoon. For starters, you don't have to be all things to your children; in other words, it's OK if you don't do something with them.

One of the things I often feel I have to do is be my child's constant playmate. So I find that when I am not working I try to make up for it, but the reality is she doesn't always need me to play with her and by interrupting her all the time when I am free (usually to assuage my guilt) all I am doing is teaching her that she needs me to play with her all the time. So be aware of what you are inadvertently teaching your kids.

Are you showing them that work makes you feel guilty, and allowing them to play on this? Are you placing work above their needs and then trying to compensate for it later? Are you doing a bad job of both your business and mothering because you can't make yourself separate the two? If so you need to step back and tell yourself the truth. Your kids are not going to suffer just because you are a working mother. And they are not going to be scarred for life because you're at the kitchen table working instead of painting with them. In fact you're not just working for your own benefit but for your family's – so stop feeling guilty.

3 DON'T ALLOW ANYONE TO MAKE YOU FEEL BAD

Ignore the newspapers that claim working mums are damaging their kids, or read the full version of the report and see if that's what they're really saying (nine times out of ten the story will have been reported badly). The fact is, everyone has his or her own ideas about what makes for good parenting, and what's right for one person needn't be right for you. What you might also find is that some people will try to impose their opinion on you. For example, you may have a disapproving relative or a friend who doesn't believe mothers should work, or a mother who feels you shouldn't be starting something new when your kids are young. What's important here is not to prove them wrong, but to do what you feel is right for you and your kids. Remember, you can't stop them trying to make you feel guilty, but you can stop yourself from feeling bad. Just remind yourself what you are doing and why.

Likewise, be aware that older children are really great at manipulating your guilt. My father ran his architectural business from our home and my brothers and I were very adept at using the fact that he felt guilty for working all the time as a way to get what we wanted. We'd only have to say, 'We never do anything fun because you're working,' and a small treat would come our way. Finally, don't allow the people that you work with to make you feel guilty. If you have to stop work at 4.00 pm because your kids are home from school or your nanny is going home, you're not shirking your responsibilities. Clients don't have the right to dictate how you choose to work, you are your own boss now and that means you can stop work whenever you want to and don't have to apologise for it or explain (although a polite reason why wouldn't go amiss if you need to smooth someone's ruffled feathers).

4 IT'S NOT MUMMY V BUSINESSWOMAN

It doesn't have to be the mummy in you versus the businesswoman in you, so don't set it up that way. Mummy guilt stems from the fact that we can't do everything that we need to do in our lives and be with our children. So whether you're in the next room working while your baby screams, or in an office, you have to accept that there are going to be times when you're going to feel bad. However, unless you are severely neglecting your child or setting a very bad example by placing work over their needs all the time, there is no reason for you to think you're doing a bad job.

Creating a business that works from home is hard work in the early stages and you need to put in 110 per cent, but don't feel bad about this because further down the line your kids will benefit from having you within their sights all day. Plus, you'll get to add to your family's income, feel a sense of achievement and build something long-lasting.

In the meantime, if you're still worried that working is detrimental to their development, it might help to know some facts about kids and working mothers. Cut this list out and pin it by your desk, so that you can look at it every time you feel guilty and remind yourself that your kids are just fine!

➤ Researchers at Bristol University, UK, studied how 12,000 children were affected by their parents' working patterns and discovered that in terms of psychological well-being and behaviour, young children with working mothers did just as well as those with mothers who didn't work.

➤ The same study found that if you're a working mum, it's also good for your kids, as dads tend to become more involved, especially in the basic functions of feeding, reading, and playing with their children.

➤ A study from the University of California found the most important factor in a child's development is not whether or not their mum goes to work but whether or not their mum is happy with her life.

➤ The Study of Early Childhood Care found that children of working mums benefited from the parent's involvement in the outside world and were more apt to cultivate their own interests, socially and academically.

➤ The same study found daughters of working mothers are also less likely to have teenage pregnancies and more likely to see higher education as a desired and necessary part of their lives. Sons benefited by learning to respect and admire women 'who can hold their own'. They also went on to be less stressed when contemplating marriage, since they felt that the full burden of household economics would not be placed solely on their shoulders. For wives, they actively sought women who had solid careers.

➤ Finally, a study from researchers at the University of Texas at Austin found no differences in children's social and intellectual development during the first three years of life between those whose mothers spent a lot of time with them in infancy and those whose mothers spent less time because they worked.

5 DON'T FORGET YOUR PARTNER

It always pays to get your partner behind you if you're going into business for yourself, not just to help out with the child-care and have a secure salary but also because starting up means a very limited social life, and lack of time for him, which can lead to one very disgruntled housemate. The way round this is to make sure that you always have at least an hour together at the end of the day, whether it's to eat dinner or simply to chat in front of the TV. Also remember: as stressed and overwrought as you may be, you also need time out from your business and childcare.

Money can become another issue, as it's likely to be tight for the first year, so make sure you keep your partner in the loop regarding business issues that affect the family and your home. Working from home can also build resentment if your partner now sees you as someone who is at home and therefore has time during the day to pick up dry-cleaning, do DIY tasks and generally be his PA alongside all your work. To combat this, lay out clear ground rules before you go into business about what your working day will be, what working for yourself will entail and how you can make this work as a family.

Finally, when you work alone it's easy to take out all your frustrations and stresses on the one main adult you see every day – your partner – avoid doing this by finding a business mentor to vent your work frustrations on, and a helpful friend to vent your domestic issues on. This way time alone together doesn't have to be about what you've done and he hasn't, and about how stressed you are.

KITCHEN TABLE TYCOON PROFILE

Leila Wilcox

Business: Halo 'n' Horns – chemical-free skincare range for children with sensitive skin

'After having a baby in 2003 I decided I needed to plan a secure future for my son. I didn't have many qualifications but I had dozens of business ideas; plus, as my dad and mum had had their own businesses I always knew that it was something I wanted to do, too. By the time my son was two years old I was desperate for a break. I knew I had the drive and ability to set up a business, I just didn't know how to start it, and so I applied to a TV programme that was looking for entrepreneurs. I got through and was teamed up with business mentors who gave me the help, confidence, and know-how to make my idea possible.

The idea behind Halo 'n' Horns was simple: my son Troy had sensitive skin that flared up after a bath, and I wanted to buy him something that was kinder to his skin. Yet, everything out there was expensive for a mum like me on a budget. So, after researching products on the Internet and talking to other mums, I realised there was a gap in the market for a range of babies' toiletries that were free from chemical nasties that parents could buy in their local super-market.

However, the start-up period was hard, even with my mentor's help. It was a real sink-or-swim situation, and even though I was working at home four days a week while Troy was asleep, I realised that I needed to give the business more time. So three days a week I decided to work in London and lived in a small room above my mentor's office. It was very stressful and hard because up until then I had been a full-time mum and wasn't used to being away from my son. Also I had no money to go anywhere so I just worked all the time.

It paid off though, because within six months I had a firm business plan, a website and a sample bottle of the product. Then, after a meeting with Tesco, I suddenly had an order for 200,000 bottles. It was brilliant and frightening all at the same time, as we had to find the money upfront to produce the bottles. Then just before delivery we discovered that some bottles were leaking so we had to check (by hand) 38,000 bottles, to make sure that they were OK and we didn't look terrible in front of Tesco. The good news was that the bottles were fine and we delivered them – within four weeks we had tripled our sales target.

It was also such a high to walk into Tesco with my mum and Troy and see Halos on the shelves – I felt so proud. Now we're in most of the large supermarket chains, I feel even more of a high now when I get emails from happy customers, and especially from mums saying that the products have helped cure their kid's eczema. In fact I still can't quite believe it when someone who doesn't even know me buys a product.

My tip to mums who are thinking of starting up is simply to go for it! Most businesses don't cost a lot to set up and there is so much expert help out there that is free. You just need to believe in yourself and do it. Also, I couldn't afford nursery or childcare during the day when I was working from home, so I asked friends with kids if they would look after my son for one day a week, and in return I'd babysit for them at the weekends. It did mean that every Friday and Saturday night I couldn't go out, but that was fine because all the hard work was worth it – Halo 'n' Horns is the best thing I've ever done!'

KITCHEN TABLE TYCOON PROFILE

Jenni Baxter

Business: Bluex2 Web Design – complete Web design service

'When our three girls were babies, my husband and I had a "business meeting" to discuss what our most important goals and dreams for our family were. Some of those goals and dreams were: to work together, to work from home (to be with the children), to be able to travel and expose our children to other cultures and to keep abreast of technology/ music, etc. (because we didn't want to wake up one day with teenage children and a huge generation gap).

About a week after that "meeting", we took a one-day course in Web design as part of our goal to keep abreast of technology – and halfway through the day it all fell into place. We loved the course, and we realised that with Web design as a business we'd be able to work together, from home, and travel. So we then signed up for various other university part-time courses related to Web design; and as soon as my husband's contract in Sydney came to an end a few months later, we moved to Noosa and set up our Web design company.

Originally, I had been a celebrity journalist in London and South Africa, interviewing up to three movie stars a week, but as stars don't visit Australia on a weekly basis, I knew I wouldn't have been able to generate a sustainable income in the same work there. My husband also needed a career change. He was working in the IT department of a merchant bank and felt that his days were meaningless, spent with people he didn't care to socialise with. Plus, if it weren't for becoming a mother, I wouldn't have changed my career path, but once I had children my dream was that I would spend 100 per cent of my time with them until they went to school. We had been lucky enough to have two years with our first child when neither of us worked (spending our entire nest egg!) – and so we knew that there was an incredible difference for the entire family between dad being home-based and dad really only being accessible at weekends.

Motherhood also made me grow up a little in terms of making money. Pre-children, I would work for free just for the love of it; but once you have children they're your priority and so you want to earn money for them, their education and their well-being. And now, every time I do something for free I realise I'm spending time on somebody else's business instead of my kids.

There are moments when I do feel horrible when work takes me away from the kids – like when they were little, the first day that a nanny arrived to look after them while I worked, I looked through the windows and wished I was the nanny out there playing with them rather than sitting in front of the computer. But guilt is not what I felt. More a sense of having to come to terms with the fact that I am a mother now with real responsibilities that go beyond my own whims, and now I need to do certain things that may not be my personal passion in order to give my children what they need most; and to do what's best for my family and not just what suits me best.

Also, I don't work because I love it more than being with my kids. I work because I want to provide my children with the best I can – which is having time together and providing for their financial needs; and therefore I don't feel any guilt. My husband and I work our hours in a way that we can spend as much time as possible with our kids, so often we'll work late at night when they're asleep. All along there are decisions you make: I've turned down overseas clients' requests to fly over to meet with them, because that would mean time away from my children; I'm currently ending a big contract because it had begun to require far too much of my valuable time, which would be better spent on smaller contracts and having more time with my children.

Although juggling work and childcare can be tricky. Sometimes it's just the mindset that's difficult: to snap out of a work thought and into a child thought. Sometimes all three girls will stand around and talk to me while I'm at the computer and I have to bite my tongue to stop myself from snapping at them, because I can't finish a sentence I'm thinking about and my head's going insane. I think school is the most difficult thing to juggle for us – because we have to wake up early to take them; and then just when you're getting into the swing of things, it's time to pick them up. We look forward to the holidays because then they're home playing and drawing while we work – and we don't have to wake up early. We're very lucky also to have my mother living nearby. She regularly picks up the girls from school so that our work day doesn't get broken, they're still having fun and my mom loves having this time with them.

Our name came quite easily to us: we call each other "Blue", so our company became Bluex2 (Blue times two). We were almost better as a start-up working intuitively than a little further down the road. In the beginning, we did a couple of friends' websites for budget prices – and they gave us the portfolio to then clinch bigger deals which, in our naivety, we charged a lot more for, which was great. But as time went along, we found out about other small Web design companies around us who charged less, so we stupidly cut our costs to attract clients – which in retrospect I regret. It just meant that we weren't able to provide as good a service any more because we were totally overworked and underpaid.

We also started off with a huge debt – so not actually getting to enjoy the profits was a low! But the personal highs have far outweighed those lows: working from home while the children were toddlers; having the flexibility to relocate to France each year for a few months (where the children go to school and we're able to see old friends). The highs of our business achievements have been working on a website from scratch to where it now has over half a million members; and getting contacted by our dream film company to create a website for them.'

KITCHEN TABLE TYCOON PROFILE

Beverley Daniels

Business: Photography – specialising in newborns, babies, children, families and maternity

'After having my son in 2002 I knew I didn't want to go back to working for someone else. I used to be a buyer for a small clothing company based out of Toronto. I worked there for many years and simply had had enough because I literally lived out of my suitcase and didn't know day to day which city I was going to be in. It was a lot of fun in my twenties but I knew it wasn't something I wanted to do for the rest of my life once I had a baby.

I had once thought that I would open my own store but all those years of retail sucked the passion out of me. On the plus side it made me look at my life and ask myself what I really wanted to do, and photography was the answer. Photography has always been my passion and so I started taking photography courses at Ryerson University in Toronto and realised that I wanted to make this my career, but I just didn't know what type of photography I was going to try to make a living from.

It was the summer of 2005 that made it all clear. A couple of women who were friends and pregnant at the same time approached me to photograph their beautiful bellies. I wasn't prepared at all – I had no studio equipment and not even a proper camera, but this didn't seem to bother them, and so I had my first booking. It all went really well, so they booked me for their newborn photo shoots. From there they told all their friends, who told their friends, and it snowballed into the business I have now.

To get things going, I first got my website up and running. As a photographer, it's important to be able to showcase your work. So I made some postcards and business cards with my work on them and put them in stores and doctors' surgeries where there would be a lot of pregnant women and women with babies and children. I also contacted stores catering for pregnant woman and babies and asked if they would be interested in showcasing my work. That way they get some nice photography for their wall space and I get free advertising. The Internet is also my best friend. I added myself to every search engine possible as well as websites that pertain to my business.

I understand that some woman don't have the choice of staying home and therefore have to hire nannies. I didn't want to do that. I didn't want someone else raising my children and I was lucky enough to have a husband who makes a good living and this therefore gave me the freedom to start my own business from home. My photography gives me something to call my own and at the same time I get to watch my children grow up before my eyes and can be the one who takes them to swimming lessons, doctor's appointments, etc., during the day and still be able to do some editing and send off print orders in the evening.

The highs for me are definitely seeing my business become a success; I love making my own hours, I love seeing the smiles on my clients' faces when I hand over their prints, and I am so happy that I am finally doing what

I always wanted to do. The lows are trying to balance it all. Between keeping the house clean, watching the kids, fitting in time with my husband and meeting my clients' needs it becomes quite a juggling act. The days are long because I can only get the bulk of my work done at night when the kids go to bed. They say motherhood alone is like two full-time jobs, so when you add a home business to the pot things can get a little hectic!

Right now I am only doing my photo shoots at the week-ends because I am home with my kids. I set up my studio every weekend in my living room and my husband takes the kids out on adventures. I plan to open up my own studio once my kids are in school full time, and that way I can take on a few more clients, too. It will be REALLY nice when I don't have to set up and take down my studio on a regular basis.

My advice to other mothers is to follow your heart. If you are unhappy with what you are doing, then go after your passion. Enjoy your kids while they are still young – they will thank you for it and you will be a much happier person.'

CHAPTER FOUR
How to get started

By now you should know if you're Kitchen Table Tycoon material, what idea you're going to run with and how to make it work from home, so now on to the basics of how to take your idea from a dream to a working reality.

Although it's good to have a vision of how your business is going to run and a belief that you will be successful, there comes a time when you have to come up with a realistic, practical and detailed business plan, not just for your business dealings, such as potential funding, but also for yourself. A good business plan will not only commit your ideas to paper but will also help you to see what you're doing, what needs to be done and what pitfalls you may have missed.

Like many mumpreneurs, when I was starting out my idea was to write from home four days a week (taking one day off), and hopefully write a bestseller and live off the royalties for life. In reality, once I wrote my business plan I realised that working out my time off and keeping my fingers crossed about a bestseller was no way to set myself up for business success. So, before you start working from home you need to establish some simple facts, such as:

1. What sets you apart from the rest of the field; that is, why is someone going to give you work or buy from you in preference to your competitor?

2. How are you going to use your USP to your advantage to get clients to keep using you?

3. Who is your market?

4. What are your short-term and long-term business goals?

Strangely enough, you may think that you are pretty clear about the above, especially if you have talked it over endlessly with friends and colleagues. This is great, but writing a business plan is essential because it will enable you to see (a) if you are clear; (b) if you are being realistic; and (c) whether or not you really do have a well-thought-out business idea.

A plan should help you to see what kind of funding (if any) you need and also help you pay attention to the details you may have skipped over, such as how to market yourself and find potential clients; not to mention how to deal with the financial aspect of your business (something many women skate over), and develop your business beyond its initial idea.

Fifteen years down the line I still have a business plan, which I update regularly, because I realise now that in order to keep moving my business forward I need to know what my goals are, where I'm heading and why. And, in a nutshell, so do you. You may be a jump-in-at-the-deep-end kind of woman, but if you want your business to succeed you have to know everything there is to know about it before you start. Which is why this chapter is all about researching everything involved, from your product to your customer, and then writing a fantastic well-thought-out business plan to map out where you're going.

How to write a business plan

When it comes to writing your own business plan, the first thing to know is that a business plan is not a document you should be scared of. It sounds frightening but it's simply a business record designed to tell you and someone else what your business is, who you are and exactly how much it's going to cost to get it off the ground. Write it correctly and it will not only help you to see who your customers are but also what your competition is, as well as any weaknesses in your business that could lead to failure. For this reason a good business plan should contain the following six elements:

1 A SUMMARY, AKA AN EXECUTIVE SUMMARY

This fancy-sounding title is vital because often it's the only section potential investors will read. In essence it is a summation of your whole business plan and should be a short, concise, passionate pitch about your business. Make it straight to the point so that it tells someone instantly what your business is and who you are. It should contain information on:

1. The kind of business you have.

2. The business's USP.

3.   Who you are and what your background is.

4.   How much funding you will need, and why.

The best way to write this part is to try to sum up your business in a sentence or two (look at your competition, or your favourite brands, and see how they are doing this). If you can't do this you need to focus your idea, as all good businesses can be sold in a sentence or less. Make sure that you also emphasise its uniqueness and why you're the best person to start it, backing up your statements with well-researched information about your product and details about your working background. This is not the place to expand lyrically about your business, so think short, think clear and think no more than a couple of pages.

2 YOUR BUSINESS

This is the section where you describe what your business is in clear and simple language, so that someone who has never heard of your service or product will get a clear and precise picture of what you are selling and why. So be sure to include:

1.   A description of what it is that you specialise in.

2.   Why you're selling your product or service. (That is, why are you needed? Are you solving a mum problem? Are you offering a unique service?)

3.   What differentiates your business from the competition (if any) out there.

4. How you are going to provide it/make it/buy it/
   import it.

If you're stuck for how to explain your business, put yourself
in the shoes of a potential customer (or investor) and think
about what you'd want to know about this business before
you bought anything or invested in it.

3 WHO'S YOUR CUSTOMER?

This is the lengthy research bit where you talk about who
your customer is and how much you know about your
market, including the competition out there or why there
is a lack of it. (See Researching Your Customer on page
126.) Your customer profile should be clearly defined so that
someone reading your plan knows:

1. Who the customer is.

2. Why the customer would buy from you.

3. What makes your business different from your competitors.

Be sure to back up everything you say with market research.

4 YOUR MARKETING STRATEGY

This is your grand plan of how you're going to conquer the
market and make a fortune (see Chapter 6 for more on this).
It's here that you should detail exactly what you're going
to do to entice customers to use your service or buy your
product. It needs to show:

1. How you will let customers know about your product or service.

2. How you will get return business, ie get customers to keep coming back to you.

Try to be as detailed as you can, and give several different tactics for marketing, such as word of mouth, PR and advertising, being sure to mention how much you intend to spend on your marketing and how exactly you're going to get PR or where you'll place advertisements.

5 THE FINANCE PLAN

This is your costings plan, and, whether you intend to employ an expert to help you here or not, you have to have a basic idea of your finances and an understanding of the financial aspects of a business. This means knowing what sales forecasts, cash flow, profit-and-loss statements and balance sheets are all about. This is essential because it's what potential investors or partners, and even suppliers, are likely to question you thoroughly about before they do business with you. (See Chapter 5 for more on this.)

This part should also map out:

1. How you will fund your business.

2. What equipment you need to start your business; for example, a computer, and so on.

3. What office supplies you will need.

6 MISCELLANEOUS SECTION

Questions to ask yourself (although these do not need to be a part of your 'official plan') are:

1. Is there enough space in my house for me to work?

2. How much money do I need for childcare?

3. If I am working around my children, is there really enough time to start a business?

4. What will my working hours be?

5. How much money do I need to make each month to maintain my living standards?

How your business plan should look

Tempting as it is to jazz up your business plan with fancy computer wizardry and elaborate fonts to impress investors or suppliers, be aware that most people are just looking for a simple layout so that they can read the information clearly. Other potential pitfalls to avoid when writing a business plan include using too much business jargon in an attempt to look more professional than you know you are (an investor will spot this a mile off) or making grand statements about your business without backing them up. The simple thing to do is to add a piece of your research for every statement you write. For example, instead of saying: 'There's a definite need for maternity wear in this area', say: 'We're filling a gap in the market for maternity clothes because within a five-mile radius of this area are X amount of young couples, X amount of nurseries and baby shops but no maternity clothes being sold.'

Also, make sure to start writing your business plan well before you start your business or start looking for investors, and definitely before you start trading, for two reasons: (a) if you haven't written a plan you're really not ready to start anything; and (b) the moment you start talking to backers or financial institutions they will ask to see your business plan. Don't be fooled into thinking you can throw one together overnight, a good business plan takes months to write, research and put together. Give yourself between two and six months to put yours together.

'All in all it took me nine months to put together a proper proposition and a brand name'.
Louise Potts, Naked Body Care

Above all be succinct. You are not writing a novel or an essay but a professional business document. This means keep to the point, don't make jokes or go off on a personal tangent but, instead, ensure that you leave the reader a good and clear idea of what you're doing.

Finally, before you send your business plan to anyone, proofread it carefully for mistakes, typos and grammatical errors. People will not take you seriously otherwise. If you can't proofread, give the document to two trusted friends and ask them what they think. Friends who could be potential customers and/or potential investors are good people to run it by first so that they can also tell you if they feel you have missed anything out.

If you still feel at a total loss about how to write a business plan, check out the Resources section of this book for helpful websites, or visit your local bank, as many have a template that you just need to fill in, and business advisers who are willing to help you. And whatever path you go down, remember: if you can't summarise your business into a business plan then your idea is not as solid and well researched as you previously thought, which means you need to go back to the drawing board before investing your time, money and energy in it.

Naming your business

'We found our name purely by accident. Friends of friends kept saying, "Oh, are you two the Homefinders?" and it just sort of stuck. When we looked on Company's House for the name it wasn't taken yet and neither were the group structure names that we wanted, such as The Homefinder Group Ltd, Homefinder Worldwide, so we registered them quick smart, then we also found that the domain names were not taken so we registered those, too!'
Freya Bletsoe, Homefinder UK

The naming game is another part of the business game that many would-be entrepreneurs love to play with. Ask around and you'll find that nearly everyone has an idea of what they'd call their business. So what should you do? Name it after yourself? Find a catchy word to hang it off? Simply make up a name you love and go with it? Well, here's a tough bit of advice: if you thought of your business name long before your actual business, it's time to do what writers do and 'kill your darlings'; meaning, change the name, because you've got it the wrong way round. Instead of making a business fit the name you have chosen, you have to make a name to fit your business.

For example, one friend has always dreamed of calling her personal training business 'Pink PT' because she had an idea for a logo and liked the ring of the name. However, aside from putting off potential male clients, the name says nothing about what she was selling, as most people don't know that PT sounds for 'personal training' and the word 'pink' indicates fluffy and girlie – not words you'd associate with fitness. Therefore, her business name is not going to help her to attract business.

CHOOSING THE RIGHT NAME

This is why naming your business should be a thought-filled process with strong reasoning behind it, because the name of your business is what will draw people to you (customers and investors) as well as making you stand out from the competition and creating the right impression for your business in the marketplace. This doesn't mean you have to be boring about it, but you do have to make sure that your business name reflects the nature of your business, does what it says on the packet and has the right ring to it. Take these examples:

Naked Body Care Beauty products that have removed the bad stuff and left the basic good stuff, hence products you want to get naked for and are naked themselves.

Boost Juice A juice that will literally give you a healthy boost.

Grobag A sleeping bag that your baby can grow into.

Babylicious Delicious baby food.

Now for some of the bad ones:

Fat Tummies A maternity shop. What pregnant woman wants to be called fat?

Rubbish Fast Food A joke by the owners, but not so funny when they went bust due to lack of customers.

When choosing your name always be sensible and don't use, or attempt to modify, a famous brand name, because their lawyers will come down on you like a ton of bricks. Think they'll never know? They will, and when they find you they will claim trademark infringement and make you rename yourself, pay their legal costs and essentially put you out of business. Also, avoid naming the business after yourself. Unless you're Julia Roberts no one wants to buy Knickers by Julia, no matter how proud you are of what you have achieved. Also, bear in mind that you might want to sell your business one day and this is less likely to happen if it's named after you.

Take the website Friends Reunited. It does what it says on the packet, everyone understands what it is when they read the name and therefore buyers were eager to purchase it because they knew it was a strong brand. Had the founders named their business 'Julie and Steve Pankhurst.com', the site wouldn't have been so successful and a buyer wouldn't have come calling and paid them millions for it.

ROAD-TEST THE NAME

Your next step is to test out the name. Whereas it's important to keep your idea a secret, in order to research your idea tell a group of selected and trusted people your business name (if you feel nervous about this you could get them to sign a confidentiality agreement first) and see:

1. If they can tell you what your business is.

2. If they can spell it (if they can't it doesn't bode well for your website).

3. If they have heard the name before.

4. What they associate with the name.

Then ask them for their thoughts on it, although bear in mind that whenever you ask a group of people to do this most people think this means they have to be critical, so take everything they say with a pinch of salt. Once you have their feedback think carefully about the name you have chosen. Does it work? Will it sell your service or product to the best advantage, or do you have to go back to the drawing board?

IS THE NAME AVAILABLE?

Finally, when you have done all the above, check the availability of the name. Is someone out there in the world already using it? You can find this out on search engines like Google and at your country's trademark, patents and copyright associations. If the name is free, consider protecting your intellectual property rights via copyright, trademark or a patent to stop a competitor from stealing it.

The difference between a patent, copyright and a trade-mark is:

➤ A patent is for something you have invented.

➤ A copyright is automatically attached to anything you have written, painted or photographed (but isn't given to ideas that haven't been written down).

➤ A trademark is for a distinctive symbol or name that identifies you; for example, the Nike tick.

Unless you have invented something like some of the Kitchen Table Tycoons in this book, such as the Cuddledry towel, all you may need to focus on is your trademark. Although be warned, you may think you don't need to do this, but the more original your idea is the more likely it is that someone will steal it, copy it and sell it, so it's up to you to protect yourself.

Researching your customer

Market research may sound like a difficult and expensive concept for a new business but, in effect, it just means gathering vital information about your customers, your competition and your product – information that will help you to achieve sales and to target your customers correctly. Knowing about your customers will make or break your business, which is why it's important to do your market research and to use it to create a strong customer profile. You will then understand who your customer is, know how to attract them and how to keep them. For example, it's useful to know:

1. Your customers' age range.

2. The areas in which they live.

3. How much they earn (so that you can work out if they can afford you).

4. What their lifestyle is like.

5. What they spend their money on.

6. If they have children.

USE A FOCUS GROUP

Put together a focus group. This is a group of people who you think are your potential customers. Ask friends and friends of friends, and/or put leaflets out in cafés and shops in areas where you think your customers live. When you have a group of about ten people, get them together and, over a cup of coffee, ask them for their opinions.

You don't have to show them your product or even tell them the specifics of your business, simply ask them what they think about similar products (use your competition as examples). For example, if you're going to start selling funky kitchen ceramics, collect together a few of the ranges that are already out there. Buy a high-end and a low-end product and ask your group:

1. What they think of the products in terms of price, design and taste.

2. Which products they would buy and why.

3. Where they shop for products. Department stores, online, locally?

4. What they want from a product like this.

5. How much they would pay.

6. What would make them go back and buy it again.

7. What it would take to get them to shop with you.

8. What would entice them to buy from you. More information, pricing, delivery?

Once you've targeted a focus group, take to the streets and approach people who you think might buy from you. You don't have to literally pace the streets. If your potential market is, for example, young urban professionals, go to places where they hang out. Ask if you can showcase your products or service at your local coffee bar on a weekend morning, for example. If you're after online customers such as new mums, try the parenting forums (although seek approval from the site before doing this).

ASK THE RIGHT QUESTIONS

Above all, when you are researching your customer, make sure you ask the right questions that will lead to more than a yes or no answer (known as an open-ended question). It's no good saying, 'Would you buy an ethical body cleanser?' as the answer will just be yes or no. Instead, ask:

➤ 'What would make you buy an ethical beauty cleanser?'

➤ 'Would price be a factor for you?'

➤ 'How could I encourage you to buy this?'

➤ 'Why wouldn't you buy it?'

➤ 'What do you buy at the moment?'

And, hard as it is, don't ask what's known as a leading question to get the answer you want. For example, if you ask, 'Would you buy a cleanser that helps children and the environment?' most people would say yes, but whether that would be a factor when they actually went shopping is another matter all together. Better to ask them:

➤ What cleanser they choose and why.

> ➤ What motivates them to choose a particular brand.
> Is it loyalty, packaging, price?

YOUR CUSTOMER PROFILE

By the end of all your research you should have a profile of who you think your 'ideal' customer is, and from this you should be able to write a description of your customer for your business plan.

For example, if you were selling organic food for pregnant women your customer profile might be as follows: My customer is a first-time mother, in her thirties who lives in X or Y. She is worried about the environment, recycles, buys the *Ecologist* and buys organic food already. She is worried about her health, and looking for healthy options. She has a network of other mummy friends, has lunch out three days a week and spends X amount on food each week. She shops locally and in the farmers' market and cooks at home but wants to make sure she's eating right.

Based on this you can do more research at your local library or on the Internet and work out how many other potential customers with this profile live in your area or are accessible to you via the Internet. Do the research and you'll be able to identify a customer base before you start, and so be able to work out a viable marketing strategy to reach them and therefore potentially make your business successful.

Research your competition

....

It's amazing how many people don't bother to look at their competition before going into business, either assuming they don't have any or that what they're going to sell or offer is way above the competition out there and so they needn't worry. This may well be true, but if your plan is to make homemade cakes and two local shops do it cheaper and don't charge for delivery, you're in trouble, even if your cakes taste a thousand times better. Doing your competitor research and market research before you set up enables you to discover if a market exists and how you'll be able to lure business away from your competitors.

So to start, you have to identify just who your competition is, where they are and how successful they are. This way you can determine whether they have a 90 per cent market share (in which case how are you going to win customers away from them?) or if they aren't capitalising on their market. Remember to use the research you already have and don't just focus on the people you assume to be your competition but also on those companies your focus group is telling you is your competition.

For example, as a homemade cake producer you may not think the big chain supermarkets are in competition with you or that they won't affect a small local business like yours, but they will if your focus group is telling you that they only shop in one place and like to buy everything from there.

Your next step is to act as a customer and call or visit the competition and do some undercover detective work. Ask how much their service or product costs, as well as questions that directly affect your business, such as delivery times, hidden costs and customer service, and even how successful they feel they are. You don't have to let on that you're starting your own business, just flatter the owner or staff about their business and you'll be surprised what they tell you. You could even be very cheeky and ask who they think their competitors are and how they feel they differ from them.

ACT ON YOUR RESEARCH

When you have all your research, look carefully at what you've found. As desperate as you are to start your own business, if all your research is telling you that there is no market out there, or the market is overcrowded with competition, don't ignore what you know. You need either to change your business angle or check your results with other reports and then adjust your business plan accordingly.

Also bear in mind that market research is something that is worth coming back to time and time again. Your first research should be done at every stage of your business, at the customer stage, the product design stage (to find out if customers like the look of your product/website/logo design) and then later at the development stage (see Chapter 6) where you can use existing customers to tell you what you can do to be more efficient at selling to them. After all, the more research you do the better you will know your customer and the more successful you will be.

Find a business mentor

'In the beginning I didn't have a mentor, which in some ways was good because I didn't actually set myself any barriers. I didn't know what I could or could not achieve. But later I had

an excellent one who helped us exactly when we needed it.'
Janine Allis, Boost Juice

One excellent way to complement your market research and work your way through a business plan is to find yourself a business mentor. Finding someone who has already been there and done that can be a fast track to success, which is why a good business mentor is a must for most Kitchen Table Tycoons. Mentors are people who can give you and your business a broader vision, and they should be empathetic and experienced business people who lend an ear to your concerns and provide guidance to help you achieve your goals. However, be aware that mentors are not people who will do all the work for you or try to take over. Mentoring is not executive coaching or business consultancy, which means your mentor will not be running the business for you or giving you endless amounts of their time. Instead they will advise, share their experience with you and help guide you.

To find the right mentor, the trick is not just to attach yourself to the nearest successful businessperson you know but to identify someone you have an instant gut feeling is right for you. Look for a mentor you admire, someone who has a similar outlook to you, and someone who has the ability to give you help, without taking over or belittling your ideas. More importantly, search for a person you respect, but are not wholly intimidated by, because it's no good having someone you are too afraid to disagree with or ask questions.

If you can't think of the ideal person, then pay attention to what's going on around you in your business sector. Look for businesses that friends are raving about, or look to see if there is a business in your sector that has suddenly gone sky high.

If there is no one who immediately comes to mind, think outside the box. Write to a well-known businessperson, and/or expert in your field and tell them you're looking for a mentor. Many successful business people already know the benefits of mentoring, and even mentor within set schemes already, so will be more willing than you might think to help.

Questions to ask possible mentors are:

1. Are they willing to mentor you? It sounds obvious, but it's best to set out the ground rules from the beginning and state that you're looking for a mentor.

2. How long have they been in business?

3. What have been the highs and lows of their business?

4. What do they think you're doing right?

5. What do they think you're doing wrong (and why)?

To get the most out of a mentoring relationship, start by getting rid of your defensive gene, because although it's good to believe in yourself you also have to be open to constructive criticism. A good mentor will challenge your ideas and thoughts, and make you stand up for your idea and beliefs – they are not there to pat you on the back.

Although it may make you feel sick inside when you hear something hard about your business or the way you're going about things, listen, think about what's being said and then make a decision about it. And remember: because a mentor has already experienced the challenges of operating and successfully developing a business, they can offer you the following benefits:

Someone to turn to Working alone is hard, there are no colleagues to bat ideas off, and no boss to crack the whip, and so a mentor can be a sounding board for your theories, ideas and plans. They are not someone telling you what to do but a guiding and supportive hand.

A chance to learn from their mistakes Their experience may have been different, but when setting up a business there are common mistakes entrepreneurs make over and over. Listen to what they have to say and learn from their experience.

An opportunity to step back from your business Step back and look at the bigger picture instead of the day-to-day aspects. A mentor can also help you to identify strengths, weaknesses and opportunities, and help you to refocus on your business goals.

Guidance against pitfalls All entrepreneurs go through highs and lows, so a mentor can caution against mistakes and help you to overcome ones you have already made.

KITCHEN TABLE TYCOON PROFILE

Wendy Shand

Business: Tots to France – an organisation dedicated to providing safe, family-friendly holiday accommodation and advice for people with babies and toddlers

'The idea for Tots to France came from a holiday in France, where my husband and I spent more time keeping our children safe from hazards – unguarded swimming pools, for example – than having a good time. We'd hired a very pretty self-catering holiday house but it was a nightmare with two small children because there were no stair gates or anything we were used to at home. When we were leaving I filled in a feedback form saying how to make it child friendly and thought, why don't people do these things? They'd have more business.

However, when I came home I had no clear idea that I would set up my own business, but I came across a card offering an online course and I decided to do it. Originally my background was in marketing and PR, then I became a primary school teacher before taking a break to have my two children, so when I started the course I didn't have Tots to France in mind at all. It was only when we had to write an essay called "The Big Idea" that I wrote about my concept of Tots to France.

I had found a "mum problem" and created a business around solving it. The idea is that Tots to France would provide holiday accommodation with all the baby and child-related kit parents take for granted at home, including safety features like stair gates and enclosed pools, so that parents can actually relax on holiday instead of working twice as hard as usual.

In fact I got halfway through the course and realised I'd had a eureka moment: I realised that the holiday-let owners would also be interested in being a part of this, as people with babies tend to travel outside of busy periods, which meant the property owners would have potential business during their slow months.

At the time I was living in Wales, and I was lucky enough to find that new local businesses were being offered grants of 40 per cent for start-up costs. So I wrote my business plan, applied for a grant and got the money. From there I got a logo and started finding holiday-let owners on the Internet. I then sent email flyers to 150 owners and ten people came back to me saying they were interested.

But just as we'd bought everything we needed, such as a laptop, my husband (who's in the air force) got posted to Portsmouth. The funding no longer covered us as we weren't living in Wales, so I had to pay it all back, plus move home and deal with setting up from our new house. It wasn't the best timing, but in a way it was a good thing because it was the kick I needed to start.

I love working from home, but I am not good at routine and detest doing the same thing every day. Initially I was working all hours, which was hard, but the driving force is that this is our future business for when my husband retires from military life.

We went live in April 2006 with nine properties, all of

which I personally viewed and vetted. Then an article in the *Sunday Times* secured my first booking within a week of starting up, and by the end of spring I had 18 more properties on my list; we now have 33 and it's climbing. By the end of 2006, the company had turned over just under £20k selling 26 weeks of holiday time, making a small profit, which was reinvested into the business for further website development.

By mid-2007, just 11 months from starting up, the company had turned over £100,000 selling more than 100 weeks' of holiday time. We now have a queue of properties waiting to be added, and the business has gone beyond what we expected. Next year we'll be able to draw an income from it, plus next January we're going to launch Tots to Italy, and if that works, we'll have a viable idea for a franchise, as we already have people interested in Spain, Australia and the US, so we're hoping to take the family-friendly holiday concept global.'

KITCHEN TABLE TYCOON PROFILE

Felicity Morgan

Business: The Organic Flower Company – suppliers of naturally grown fresh, seasonal flowers

'My business, the Organic Flower Company, is primarily an online florist specialising in the sourcing of organically and ethically grown flowers, delivered next day, nationwide. We have been trading since March 2006. I started the business in response to features in the press regarding the flower farming methods that were being used, particularly in South America and Africa – areas from which I had been importing flowers for use in my shop.

My previous work background had been with MBNA, the credit-card company, then as a flower importer and then as a florist. MBNA gave me a brilliant customer-service background as well as people-management skills. When I had children I worked closer to home as an administrator in the business of importing flowers. Here I learned about the flower industry and how it works from "field to front room", and later as a florist with my own shop – the real nitty-gritty of what to do with the flowers and how to make them look their best.

I thoroughly enjoy running my business from home as it has made life easy in terms of splitting the day for the children. I start really early, check emails and orders, and reply to anything urgent, stop for breakfast and to take the children to school, continue working and finish in time to collect them again. The downside is that it is virtually impossible to "switch off", and if the phone rings it could be my grand-mother or it could be a potential business customer from South America!

The high point of being my own boss has been the empowerment and freedom, the feeling of forging ahead on a solo mission into entrepreneurship. The downside being that on less brave days I feel completely isolated, vulnerable, convinced that the phone will never ring, that I have too much responsibility and that I am desperate to impress new clients but should have collected the children from their gym club ten minutes ago (which I forced them to go to against their will because I needed that extra hour!).

If I had to do it all again I would change very little. The main thing for me is that I would have sought help earlier in the form of someone to do things like driving, delivering and everyday office work – the things that are really vital but that anyone can do. I have wanted to hold the reins of my business for far too long and have ignored offers of help because I think that I am the only person capable of doing the job properly. What I can see now is that, actually, anyone is capable of putting stamps on envelopes and posting them, of delivering boxes to a nearby village and of answering the phone with a pleasant manner.

I am just about to move to "new" premises. My staff there will help me to hold the reins, which will mean, in time to come, that when I am not at "work", I will be at home with my children, safe in the knowledge that my team will be taking care of our customers' needs.'

KITCHEN TABLE TYCOON PROFILE

Barbara Cox

Business: Nutrichef – healthy meals, healthy snacks and healthcare products

'I've been a nutritionist for almost ten years, having first become interested in healthy eating while living in Japan – a country with an abundance of healthy food and relatively low rates of cancer, heart disease and obesity. I originally went to Japan to teach English and one of my students owned an exclusive restaurant called Yumeya ("house of dreams"). I worked in the kitchen to see what it would be like and learned to make Japanese dishes such as sushi, miso soup and okonomiyaki (a healthy "pizza"). As well as transforming my cooking skills, I qualified as a nutritionist. With both these strings to my bow, and with a return to the UK in mind, I set about creating a meal plan that would incorporate the important nutritional features of a Japanese diet yet appeal to Western consumers.

On my return to the UK I set up my own private nutritional therapy clinic and at the end of each consultation with clients I gave them all the recipes they would need to cook healthily for themselves for the following 30 days. I then told the client I'd see them in a month to assess the results.

The idea of giving clients the recipes was great in theory, but it just didn't work out in practice. Clients found it difficult to follow the 30-day plan, as the preparation of meals was time-consuming and the ingredients weren't always available. However, it wasn't until a frustrated client phoned me from Tesco one evening to say that they couldn't find "spelt flour" or "quinoa" that I began pondering an idea: I order the ingredients, find a chef to prepare the meals and get my husband to deliver them direct to customers' homes. And so the idea of Nutrichef was born!

To start with we did all the work on the business and the cooking from home, which was hard and fun but, due to demand, we soon realised that we'd need to find bigger premises and build our own industrial kitchen. So we re-mortgaged our house, and also looked for suitable business partners – people who could contribute business experience (which we lacked) and a bit more money. As it turned out, we had to look no further than two customers: Penny and Nigel Mason. They just loved the programme and how it was helping them with their own health challenges. After being on the meal plan for just four weeks, both of them had lost the excess pounds they were carrying around, they felt a lot more energetic and people were commenting on how much younger and healthier they were looking.

In many ways I am not surprised that we're successful. With the hectic lives that people lead nowadays, they don't always have to time to shop for and prepare healthy meals, so Nutrichef really fulfils a need.

And after three years we are just beginning to make a profit, and, through franchising, the future for Nutrichef looks very promising.

The highs for me have been getting our first customer, building our state-of-the art industrial kitchen, and being asked to be guest speaker on a radio programme. However, the number-one high without a doubt is being told by clients about the many ways that we have given them a new lease of life.

The lows have been the small numbers of customers around Christmas and the Easter holidays, which gave us a few financial scares! I remember not having enough money to get our boiler fixed, so we had to go round to a friend's house for a bath! And working long hours often means there's an imbalance between time spent at home and at work. David and I worry that our children will suffer, but, fortunately, due to the help we've had from a couple of wonderful au pairs, both our kids seem to be doing really well.'

KITCHEN TABLE TIPS FROM BARBARA COX OF NUTRICHEF

1. Stay on top of the detail and be organised.

2. Get help doing cleaning, ironing and gardening.

3. Look after your health – I'm sure my healthy diet gives me the energy to work such long hours.

4. Have some free time for yourself.

5. Don't take your eye off the big picture(s) – your

goals for your business, your goals for your family life, and your goals for the community.

6. Set goals that are achievable.

7. Believe in yourself and have confidence.

8. Learn and keep learning.

9. Admit when you make a mistake and set it straight.

10. Failure is not an option when you're 100 per cent committed!

CHAPTER FIVE
Practicalities and cash

'Cash flow is king. You really need to know your financial model
and make sure it's profitable. If you can and if you are with a
husband/life partner, try to keep one of you working and
getting an income. Businesses take a long time to get established and are very, very cash hungry, and yet life still needs
to go on. It's very hard on a young business to sustain two
large salaries.'
Janine Allis, Boost Juice

If you've never run your own business before, or are simply
someone who finds budgeting your bank account a nightmare, it's likely the financial aspect of your business is one
you have either ignored or skated over. Whereas it's tempting
to put your head in the sand and hope you can hire an expert
to sort it all out for you, it pays to understand the financial
side of how your business works. The good news is that no
matter how bad you are at financial things, with a bit of
know-how it is possible to work out a financial plan and
stick to it like any other business owner.

Of course you may be thinking that you're someone who
doesn't have to focus on this because you're not in it for

the money. However, even if you're lucky enough not to be dependent on your business to make ends meet, if you're starting a business it's essential to be serious about the financial aspects of being a business owner. This is because running a business has long-term financial implications for you and your family, which will come back to haunt you if you don't focus on the lifeblood of your business: money and profit. Also bear in mind that once you start trading, other businesses will be depending on you to do well; that is, your suppliers, which means that if you're not going to focus on the finances for your benefit, do it for the people working for you.

Lastly, whereas it's perfectly fine to go into business for other reasons besides money, such as ethical and moral reasons, as well as to fulfil a dream, without having your finances in order all those other reasons will be wasted, as will your business idea. So, before you do anything else, do your sums properly and make sure your figures add up so that you don't overestimate the cost of going it alone or underestimate what's going to be expected of you in terms of making a profit.

Working out your start-up costs

'If I had to start over I wouldn't do anything differently because I've had to learn these lessons to be where I am now. If I'd had a really good accounts person at the start I probably wouldn't understand the accounts like I do now. I don't have accounts training, but I can sit with the best of them and know what I am talking about now.'
Janine Allis, Boost Juice

Inadequate funding is one of the main reasons small businesses fail, which is why you should not underestimate your start-up costs. As a writer working from home I was sure I didn't have any start-up costs, as I already had a computer. Then I realised that I needed a fax machine (this was 1992), business cards, headed paper, an email account, money to pay my accountant and money to pay for a business banking account, and cash to survive on until I got paid for my first job. All in all I needed a lot more than I thought to survive the first year of my business (and that was without a large mortgage and a baby). So, if you're currently thinking that you don't need much, it's time to put pen to paper.

Start-up costs are, in a nutshell, the money you need to set up and run your business for at least a year; for example, computer equipment, the costs of having something manufactured, anything you need to buy to set your business up and the cost for experts such as accountants or PR help. Contrary to popular belief there are more costs to setting up a business from home than buying a laptop, creating a webpage and handing out business cards, so be very realistic about what you budget for, what you have to spend and how much you have to live on, or else you could be living hand to mouth for a while. The best way to work out your costs is to:

1. Do it in advance of setting up. This sounds obvious but many people do it the other way around and work on a I'll-wait-to-see-what-I-need basis.

2. Write it all down (see below) and then seek advice from either a business mentor or a financial expert.

WHAT YOU MIGHT NEED

Below is a list of some of the things your business might need. You may find you don't need to budget for any of it, but the list is there to make you aware of what you need to think about in terms of start-up costs.

Computer equipment

Will you need to buy a new computer or have an upgrade to your existing one? Have you budgeted for broadband, wireless and programs you might need? Should you buy a laptop rather than a desktop, or both? What about a printer and scanner? Are you going to go with a free email account or buy a domain name and set up a website? If you're about to go into business, these are questions you can't afford to ignore. So, budget for a good computer, and also for technical support; that is, someone to advise you on all of the above and also come round if your computer crashes.

Other technology

Will you need a separate mobile phone, PDA (personal digital assistant) or BlackBerry for your business? (Although bear in mind that a good mobile phone will allow you to access your emails when you're out as well as do all the things a PDA does.) If so, work out with your phone provider good rates that will save you money for calls, texts and picture messaging. How about a separate home phone line or fax line? Not to mention an answering service if you're not around.

Marketing

Do you need business cards, money for advertising and PR, headed paper and a logo designed and printed? How about flyers or a professional website designed, hosted and maintained for you? Even if you're going to print everything yourself, have you factored in how much paper you'll need, how much the ink will cost, whether you will go for colour or regular black printing. How about advertising: have you checked how much it really costs for advertising in print or on the radio, or are you assuming a figure?

Banking

Firstly, you need a business account, and these come with charges for everything from borrowing to withdrawing money. Secondly, how are your customers going to pay you? If you're selling a product you need to be able to accept credit-card payments and will have to pay for this service. Credit-card accounts generally have an initial cost for equipment plus monthly fees or minimums for the service.

Expert and consultancy services

You may not think you need ongoing accounting help, but with taxes and other state and local taxes to keep abreast of it pays to have one on hand to help you. Alongside this you may decide you need PR help – and don't forget computing, design and legal help.

Ongoing expenses

Your next step is to work out what is a one-off expense and what is an ongoing expense. Also, calculate what home expenses you have so that you can determine what you can take out of the business as a salary, although bear in mind that many new businesses don't pay a salary for the first year, so you need to factor in how much you'll need to survive on until you can afford to pay yourself.

One-off start-up costs	Cost
Equipment (stock, materials)	
Initial outlay of equipment you need for production	
Inventory	
Advertising and PR	
Consultancy fees	
Stationery	
TOTAL	

Ongoing expenses	Cost
Salary (you'll pay yourself each month)	
Supplies	
Utilities	
Taxes	
Consultancy fees	
Stationery	
Postage	
Internet/telephone	
Mobile phone	
Insurance (if applicable), ie maintenance costs for equipment	
Miscellaneous	
TOTAL	

Home expenses	Cost
Mortgage/rent	
Childcare	
Essentials such as food and travel	
Gas	
Electricity	
Telephone	
Water	
Insurance	
Council/state tax	
Credit-card/store-card payments	
Loan payments	
Home supplies (essential products)	
Miscellaneous (other money owed)	
TOTAL	

If the figures above have shocked you and made you worry about going into business, be aware that the financial impact of starting a business scares everyone, and at first the figures of what are outgoings and borrowings look frightening compared to what's coming in. However, if you have a great business idea, in time these figures will reverse themselves. In the meantime, be honest about how much you need to borrow to survive and make your business work.

Before borrowing ask yourself: can you go out less, buy less, live off cash not credit, go to the library instead of buying books, cut out the gym membership and generally change your lifestyle? You may be screaming, 'NO WAY!' but if you are determined to start your own business these are the tricks that get you there. Ways to cut back on your home and business expenses before you start are to look at who you're paying and how much you're paying. Studies show that people could save money on their insurance, utility bills, mobile phone bills and broadband accounts by shopping around for a cheaper supplier. These days it's easier to do than you think, just go to one of the many Internet companies that happily do it online for you.

Next, work out how much you owe. Include debts, such as store cards, overdrafts and money owed. Once you have a figure for money owed, be honest with yourself: can you really afford to go into business for yourself, or should you work on paying back your debts first?

Funding your business

'I funded my business Halo 'n' Horns with a £15,000 personal investment and £30,000 from a business partner. I borrowed part of this money from my nan and granddad, and more from other members of my family. That made it very personal, and meant that I was determined not to let them down.'
Leila Wilcox, Halo 'n' Horns

Now you know how much you need, you have to find some funding. There is a variety of ways to go about this and not all entail tying yourself to a financial institution. According to a study by Microsoft, 54 per cent of entrepreneurs rely on personal savings to start up, 18 per cent use bank finance, 14 per cent rely on family and friends and 6 per cent use grants. Whichever path you choose to go down, a solid and well-thought-out business plan will help you secure the money you need.

USE YOUR SAVINGS

Before you do this, ask yourself what your family would do if this amount of money was lost and not recuperated by your business. If you can afford to lose it (which hopefully you won't) go ahead and finance yourself. However, make sure you set up a business account and keep your business financial life separate from your personal finances.

DO IT ON YOUR CREDIT CARDS

It's an unwise decision to use your credit cards to fund your business. The interest rate is exorbitant and, as most companies don't make a profit in the first year, you'll be paying only minimum repayments and tying yourself to a credit-card company for a long time. Also, a business loan is cheaper in the long run and comes with less anxiety.

BORROW FROM FRIENDS AND FAMILY

Many Kitchen Table Tycoons take this route. If you do, make sure you draw up a contract stating whether the money is in return for a share in your company, or simply a gift, or if you will be repaying the loan. If you're repaying it, ensure the contract details over what time period, with or without interest and any other stipulations attached to the loan.

GET A GRANT

Look to see what your local council/state are offering new businesses, and also what national companies, charities and government organisations can offer you. Certain organisations help fund businesses for women, others for young entrepreneurs, some for businesses that are to do with certain areas such as the environment.

FIND AN INVESTOR

These are usually other business people who are willing to invest in your business for a share of the profits, although, be warned, they will also want a say in your business and some control over how you run it. If you're going to borrow from an investor, make sure you're on the same page for your business and also have a contract stipulating what's expected before you use the money.

APPROACH A FINANCIAL INSTITUTION

A bank or building society is an option for you to approach for a business loan. The pluses of doing this are that they can loan you a large amount and offer you business help alongside. The downside is that the loan is likely to come with penalties if you miss a repayment, a high interest rate and is also likely to be secured against your property; meaning, that if you default on the loan, the bank could take your house.

START WITH NO CAPITAL

This is very risky and, while some small start-ups can manage it, if you're planning to go down this route it may be wise to have another source of income at the same time, so that you can buoy up your business with a salary, then at a later date opt to do it full time.

PRICING YOUR SERVICES/PRODUCTS

'I was so keen to find customers that I didn't price myself correctly. I didn't charge for travel costs and also ended up paying extra at the printing stage to get the book to look better, which I should have really passed on to the customer. It made me toughen up and charge properly.'
Louise Millar, Memoir Publishing

Although knowing your costs will help you to decide whether you can afford to go into business or not, and what you need to borrow, pricing yourself correctly and knowing what you're going to charge your customer and why will help you to work out if your business can survive and make a profit.

If you are too cheap or too expensive compared to your competitors (and if you don't know what your competitors are charging you need to go back to the drawing board) you may well be doing yourself out of business, customers and profit.

So, if you have purposefully made your product or service expensive to capture the luxury end of the market, you need to ask yourself:

➤ What makes you think customers would prefer to opt for a premium product or service when a cheaper one is available?

➤ Do you know how to reach this market and sell to it?

➤ Are you aware that you will be working on a 'sell a little for a lot' basis, which means you'll have to work harder to sell, and the expectations for your product or service from your customers will be higher?

➤ Do you have a back-up plan if you don't sell the required amount each month?

➤ Are you strong on customer services, as the higher the price the higher a customer's expectations will be?

➤ If you're pricing yourself at the budget end of the spectrum, where you expect to sell a lot cheaply and very quickly, you need to make sure that:

1. As a start-up you are able to cope with the pace of your sales.

2. That you can cope with losing customers when you put up your prices (and all businesses have to do this).

➤ Also, if you're cheaper than the rest of the field, are you really able to make a profit while selling so low, or are you simply undercutting your competitors to find customers (in which case not making sound business sense)?

For a large catch of customers and a good chance that they'll return and give you more business, price yourself in the middle of the field. This allows you to offer discounts, up your prices and pull in potential customers from far and wide; although, be aware that it may take you longer than the budget seller or luxury-end seller to have a steady cash flow.

Don't undervalue yourself
Before you price your product or service it's worth knowing that most women business owners undervalue what they are

doing and so underprice themselves in their first year, so make sure you value yourself enough to charge properly. To get your correct price ask yourself how much money and time have you put into a product to get to the point of sale. For example, if you were going to sell cakes:

1.   How much did the ingredients cost?

2.   How long did it take you to make them?

3.   How much energy was used to bake them?

4.   How much was the packaging and delivery?

How much could you charge based on the above that would give you a small profit and still get your customers to come back to you instead of your competitors? Next, look at what your competitors are charging and why. Can you price yourself competitively within this market and still make a profit in the long term? (That is, don't undercut your competitors without considering whether you can make a profit.) Lastly, think about how much your customer is willing to pay. It's no good coming up with a figure that works for you if your customer base thinks it's too high. This is where your market research will come in handy. Think back to your focus group and what they said about how much they would pay for a product, but also what their behaviour showed you about what they actually paid.

Is the price right?
All in all your pricing needs to be adequate, so that in the long term your sales will cover:

1. The costs of starting up

2. The cost of running your business

3. The costs of developing your business

4. Profit

5. Taxes

6. Insurance

7. Holiday and sick leave

Cash flow, profit and loss

The important thing to get to grips with is the fact that money is going to be tight for at least six months to a year, even if your business really takes off, simply because it takes time for your sales/work to pay off your start-up expenses and your ongoing monthly expenses. This is why projecting your cash flow is vital to your success, because even if you have plenty of sales/work lined up, if you're not going to get paid for three months or more, you're not going to survive because you won't have any cash to make the business work.

With a cash-flow forecast (a spreadsheet showing you how much will be going in and out of your business each month) you will be able to work out if you need more initial funding, whether your idea works financially and what changes you might need to make to increase your cash flow each month. Remember that with limited cash flow all your decisions about marketing, advertising, producing and growing are also going to be limited.

It's also important to realise that cash is not profit. Just because 20 people buy your product or service at £20/$20 each, the total of £400/$400 is not a profit. You cannot even begin to think about a profit until you have deducted your overheads, start-up costs and repayments on loans. This means that you may not be able to pay yourself a salary for a while, so you also need to make sure you have enough funding/savings to cover your personal expenses before you start up.

MAKE A FORECAST PLAN

Even though no one expects you to be profitable right away, you need to put together a profit-and-loss forecast plan for your first year of business. This shows the projected financial movement of your business over a one-year period and should outline how you are going to become profitable. You can do this by working out how much you're likely to make from sales/work in a year, how much you're likely to spend, how much money you'll draw as an income and how much tax you're likely to pay. The net profit will be the money you have left once you have paid back all these overheads (gross profit is the figure before overheads have been taken off), and retained profit is the profit going back into the business.

An example of a profit and loss forecast for a company would be:

Sales in year	20,000
Less: cost of sales	(5,000)
Gross profit	15,000
Less: business overheads	(1,550)
Net profit	13,450
Less: income	(10,000)
Retained profit	3,450

Within your financial plan you should also be able to say how you plan to make this profit (for more on this see Chapter 6), so that investors know you're going to be a profitable business, and how long it will take you to realise a profit.

Managing your money

'My advice to other women setting up is to put a price on your service, your time and your experience, and keep your accounts in order, but don't try to do it all yourself or you'll get bogged down with the small stuff and lose sight of the bigger picture.'
Jenni Baxter, Bluex2 Web Design

Unlike your personal accounts, once you're up and running you need to learn to manage your business accounts effectively, not only for tax purposes but also for the future development of your business. Living in financial chaos and not knowing how much money is coming in, or even seeing payments as profit, is a disaster waiting to happen.

This means that you have to do your best to keep your costs down. Don't worry so much about what others think. To run a business you don't need flashy equipment or a special desk in your home, or a state-of-the-art mobile phone or even a website that does fancy things. Go for the essentials that you need, and which ensure your business looks good without costing the earth. Shop around for logos, headed paper and Web designers – a massive difference in price and savings can be made everywhere if you search for it.

At the same time, make sure you make cuts in the right areas. For example, it's no good creating a website that doesn't work properly, or telling suppliers and customers that you don't have an email address, don't have a mobile number or don't take credit cards – it will just make them go elsewhere. The key is to make it easy for people to contact you, find you and buy from you, without spending all your cash.

If you have your accounts in order you should always know how much money your business has in the bank, how much you owe and what's owed to you. This way you'll have a clear idea of your projected turnover and know whether you have to tweak the business to make it work, or are fully on track. Above all, hard as it is, don't be put off by your financial fore-casts and plans, unless of course the figures really don't work. Help yourself by seeking the advice of experts such as business bankers, accountants and small-business advisers and ask for support from friends and family. Being a Kitchen Table Tycoon is hard, but that doesn't mean you have to go through it alone. And finally, remind yourself: all entrepreneurs (no matter how wealthy) find the financial and personal risk of starting their own business daunting, which means you're in good company.

10 FINANCIAL TIPS TO HELP KEEP YOUR BUSINESS IN ORDER

1. Keep a daily record of your business outgoings and incomings.

2. File your receipts and invoices weekly.

3. Make sure you get paid on time and pay your bills on time.

4. Speak to your accountant about the most effective way to organise your receipts, such as under categories or by month.

5. Know what's deductible from your expenses and what isn't.

6. Keep a tax account where you automatically place money for your savings and tax.

7. Declare earnings outside of your business.

8. Find out what you can declare against tax for using your home for business place.

9. Be ready to chase up late invoices. Remember: it's not about being nice, it's about your business surviving.

10. Before you sign any loan agreement, make sure you know what's being asked for in terms of collateral. Are you willing to put your home on the line for your business?

KITCHEN TABLE TYCOON PROFILE

Janine Allis

Business: Boost Juice – smoothie and juice bars

Janine Allis is the mother of three boys aged sixteen, ten and eight, and since 2000 has been the MD and founder of Boost Juice – the largest and fastest growing juice-bar company in the southern hemisphere, which has outlets in more countries than any other juice bar.

'I had a very diverse career before starting Boost Juice Bars. From the age of 16 onwards I was everything from a media assistant for an advertising agency, to a camp leader with the Camp America programme and even a stewardess on David Bowie's yacht. Which is why when I was 34 years old and had just had my third son I decided that I didn't want to go back to work for someone else any more. I wanted to be creative, and I realised that the only way to do that was to start my own business. The only problem was I didn't have a clear idea of what I wanted to do and I had never run my own business, so I was basically starting from scratch.

As I wasn't sure what business I wanted to go into I decided to accompany my husband on a trip to the USA and investigate any emerging trends. I decided on a juice bar after noticing that there were no real healthy fast-food options for people like me with kids in Australia. I came home and wrote a business plan with my husband, which was a bit devoid of figures because that bit felt scary, and then I started consulting nutritionists and naturopaths, and came up with a menu of juices and smoothies that were healthy and free of artificial flavours and colours. I then made the recipes in my kitchen and had a juice and smoothie fest where everyone who came over tried a new concoction.

For financing, my husband and I then got a number of friends together to invest in us and we opened our first store in the city of Adelaide. Initially I did everything from paint the floor of the store, to put on a T-shirt and make the juices, but overall I was lucky to have a good, passionate manager who ran the store. This worked well because it allowed me to focus on the growth of the business from my home-town (Melbourne), instead of being tied to the day-to-day running of the store in another state, and within a year we had five more outlets. Then we landed a huge contract and, because we needed money to expand into 25 more stores across the country in just 12 months, we took a huge risk, sold our family house for capital and moved the family into a rental and worked out of there.

It was hard work and stressful but it worked so well that it soon got to the point where running the business from home took over the entire house and we ended up sleeping in the same room as our children. In the first year we lost $34,000 which was pretty amazing considering we were opening all those stores, and then in the second year we made about $500,000 and Boost really grew from there. Now we have 180 stores in Australia and we own about 30 of them outright; the rest are franchised. We decided to take this route because we wanted really fast growth, and there is no way that we could have achieved that on our own.

Overall I think I have an anything-is-possible attitude – that's been one of my best assets. So many times, particularly through building our stores, there have been "cannots" that I've converted into "can dos", as I really believe that there is a solution to every problem, especially if you have a positive attitude. My advice to anyone who wants to start their own business is, although there is plenty of reward and flexibility to being in control of your own destiny, you have to expect challenges, problems and sleepless nights as well as fear and happiness.

One of the great things for me is that my husband worked, so when I started my business although things were a little tighter with money than before it was a sacrifice that we were prepared to take. Also, I think, as a woman, don't believe you can do it all. I may have three children, a business and a husband, but the reality is that I am very lucky because I have a mum who comes to my house every single day to help out, and has done so ever since the children were little.

What you can take out of the Boost story is that your background or your education doesn't matter, the information for starting a business is all out there, and you just have to find it and then get on with it! Also, if you're working from home, be honest with yourself and others, and remember it's OK if your house gets dirty while you're busy with family and work. Finally, remember to kiss your partner and kids every day. They'll always be there – your business might not!'

KITCHEN TABLE TIPS FROM JANINE ALLIS OF BOOST JUICE

1. Have a business plan – that's vital.

2. Try not to go into business with a partner if you can avoid it.

3. Try to find mentors who have achieved success in the past.

4. Don't do it just for the money, because as soon as you do you make decisions based on that.

5. Always maintain your honesty and integrity, and do business only with people who have the same integrity and honesty that you have.

KITCHEN TABLE TYCOON PROFILE

Nadine Hill

Business: The Dream PA – virtual personal assistant

'Until I started my own business, I worked for ten years in public relations, which meant that after I had my daughter I went back to work from 9.00 am to 5.30 pm and it was exhausting. I'd feel guilty about leaving on time, and guilty because when I got home I had only an hour with my daughter, so I realised this wasn't the way I wanted to work. I knew I needed a change but I also knew I needed to contribute to the family income, so when I came across a magazine article on virtual assistants who worked for other businesses from home, I realised that my skills as a PR could easily translate into being a virtual PA.

It sounds crazy but I have always been someone who goes to sleep with ideas running around my head, and I actually woke up with the name for my company: The Dream PA. I wrote it down, and thought, yes that's it, and went on to buy the domain names and set up my site. I then handed in my notice, joined a local networking group for people starting their own businesses, and started working from home with a laptop bought on a credit card, and a hundred pounds in capital. It was a giant leap and, in a way, scary, because at a time when I had new responsibilities I was leaving the security of a full-time job, but I knew I had to do it in order to juggle family with work more successfully.

Networking locally helped me to get my first clients on-board because it raised my profile, and my reputation spread by word of mouth. However, I'd never run a business before and it was a steep learning curve. Initially, I started out with the idea that I could be a PA and support any kind of business, then I quickly realised that I was better suited to small businesses that had no admin support, so now I have more of a niche market and target sole traders. Networking also helped me to see that whereas it's good to have a vision, very often your market will dictate what you do, so you have to be flexible and adapt. For instance, my aim was to work from home, yet I have two clients where it makes more sense to work at their place, so I do.

After two years in business I now have 65 clients, which is fantastic, and as I work on an hourly basis when they need me, it means I can choose my own schedule and so be there for my daughter, whether it's for doctor's appointments, sports days or just in the house when she gets back from nursery.

If I had to do it all over again, the only thing I'd change is the way I funded my start-up. After leaving my job I realised very quickly that I didn't have enough clients to make it work. Even though it was necessary to jump out of my safety zone and just do it, I wasn't making enough to generate an income and it was a struggle. It took a good year for my business to get going and it was a bit hand-to-mouth at times, so in retrospect I should have really got some financial advice and a business loan, instead of relying on my savings and limited resources. It would have given me some much-needed breathing space and made things a lot easier. It's a tip worth knowing because businesses always need time to take off so you have to have financial backing in place.

But by far my biggest tip is to believe that you can do it. If you don't sound confident people aren't going to buy into you. It's a hard one because I wasn't like that in the beginning. I am not a natural sales person but you can learn to be. Just don't let your confidence be knocked by letting others dictate the terms of your work. And above all it doesn't matter if you make mistakes or have doubts – we all do. There are times when I am at home and I wish there was someone to talk to or spin ideas off, but on the whole I love working for myself and being at home, so really my life couldn't be better.'

KITCHEN TABLE TYCOON PROFILE
Sandra McClumpha
Business: Fake Bake UK – the UK and Continental Europe dealership for American Fake Bake tanning products

'I was never into make-up or hair or anything like that, so it came as some surprise to me when, at 16 years old, I decided I wanted to be a hairdresser and got a job in a local salon. When the owner of the salon left, I quit as well and went to work in the marketing department of a beauty-products company. After three years there I was offered promotion, but it would have meant moving from Scotland to England so, at the age of 25, I borrowed £5,000 from my parents and opened a nail and tanning salon.

I thought nails would be the next big thing, and though I had to work really hard at it, it became the best salon in the area. By the age of 32, I had six staff, but the work involved long hours, and when I had my first child I decided it was time to reassess my life and find something that fitted in more easily with motherhood.

I looked around and decided that, with the growing demand for fake-tan products, there was room for someone new in the market. So, after trying out about 20 tanning products from around the world, I tried Fake Bake, which stood out from the rest because the cream was a dark-brown colour instead of being clear or cream.

I called the manufacturers and asked for some samples, then tried out Fake Bake on my staff. The girls in the salon didn't tan naturally because they were typical Scottish girls with white skin, freckles and red hair. So I thought, if I can tan them I can tan anyone. The effect was just amazing. I was convinced that I had found a product to rival St Tropez, the main product on the market in the UK, so I flew to America to ask Fake Bake's manufacturers if they would give me the distributorship for Britain and Continental Europe. However, they refused, saying I would have to prove myself first.

I returned home determined to rise to the challenge and realised that it would be impossible to commit to both selling Fake Bake and running my salon – as well as looking after my small child – so I sold the salon for £120,000. Despite having no guarantee that my interest in Fake Bake would ever amount to anything, I got to work drumming up enough sales for Fake Bake to prove I was capable of taking on the distributorship.

I set up a makeshift office in a bedroom at home and used the money I had made from selling the salon to employ a public-relations company to promote Fake Bake. At this point I became pregnant again, but as I had no income I had little choice but to keep on working.

Luckily Fake Bake came top in a comparison test of tanning products in a magazine, and the phone began to ring with enquiries from customers, so I knew I was on to a good thing.

I started importing Fake Bake products from the US manufacturers, but at first had nowhere to store them. So I begged people I knew who ran tanning salons to take the products on a sale-or-return basis so that I had somewhere I could send people to buy them.

My self-belief and determination paid off, because after three months I was at last given the distributorship for Fake Bake in Britain and Continental Europe. My company, Fake Bake UK, is now set to have a turnover of £4.5m and has 25 staff and three training schools.

My advice for budding entrepreneurs is simple: research your market and know your competition, because that gives you an edge. And don't expect to make any money for the first couple of years if you are really serious about it.

I put the secret of my success down to the belief and sheer determination that I could combine running a successful business with raising a family. Women can lose a lot of confidence and identity when they have children. And I've been determined not to do that. Running your own business from home can be done. If I am happy, my children are happier. You can have it all.'

CHAPTER SIX
Getting your business going

You've sorted out your childcare, found your funding, rewritten your business plan about a hundred times and at last you feel ready to open the doors of your business. After all the hard work you've put in it's easy to believe that from here on in all you have to do is open up and your customers or clients will be buying from you in droves. It's an assumption that every new business owner has, and one that usually ends in disappointment unless you know how you're going to attract business to you (that is, how you're going to market your business) and how you are going to make sure your business survives for the long run (that is, what your business vision is for the future).

When most people start out they are clear about how to attract business initially and how to persuade people to buy from them or to employ them. However, many new business owners are more than a bit flaky about their pricing and about how they are going to let their business evolve after that point. Price-wise, never let others – such as your competitors and clients – dictate how much you are paid. Make a valued decision (see Chapter 5) and stick to it, remembering that you don't have to justify your prices to anyone but yourself. As for making your business grow, it's essential to have a marketing plan that tells you how you're going to attract business and which goes beyond the start-up period, so that you can keep attracting new business as well as keeping that which you already have.

Do it correctly from the beginning and you'll avoid sleepless nights and start-up exhaustion, as well as being able to plan your workload in a more consistent manner, which allows you to reap the benefits of working from home. So, before you jump in, be clear in your mind about everything, from how you're going to find customers and market yourself to how you see your business growing and growing. It may feel like just more work before you've even opened shop, but believe me you won't regret it.

Getting to grips with marketing

'As a life and personal coach, more than 50 per cent of my time, like most coaches, is devoted to marketing my services. The catch-22 is that most coaches know precious little about marketing and so are unable to generate and sustain much business. As a result, many end up quitting out of frustration and lack of motivation. I am not a natural at marketing so this is an area I have had to really work at.'
Melissa Roske, Wheels in Motion Coaching

A friend recently had the idea to set herself up in business selling some of the gorgeous knitted hats that she had a talent at making. She spent a month knitting a collection of 20 hats, designed her own website, printed up some flyers – which she gave to friends to pass out to everyone they knew – and then sent emails round all her friends and family asking them to pass it on, then waited. After two weeks she got one sale through a family member; after three she discounted her hats; and after four weeks she worked out that although she'd sold all 20 hats she hadn't made a penny and was giving up her new business. Her 'business' failed on many levels, but most of all on the idea that she could just set up a website, email a few people only once, and expect the news to spread through word of mouth using family and friends, and that business would come flooding in.

Likewise, email is not a fantastic marketing tool. This is because the total email volume worldwide is almost 200 billion messages a day, which translates into every person on earth receiving more than 30 messages every day, 70 per cent of which is spam. So, if this is your marketing method you're simply going to get lost in the crowd. Finally, to have a word-of-mouth approach to your business you have to make sure your company is known over a wide area – and that means doing it yourself, not just handing out flyers to friends. My friend should have made herself known in all the local markets, placed her hats in local shops, tried to get her hats featured in magazines and newspapers and even tried to have someone who was well known wear them – as well as having a website and flyers.

The moral of this story is: if you want to sell, sell, sell you have to work out the most effective way to inform your potential customers that you exist, and, secondly, you have to know how to position your product or service in an appealing manner so that people want to come to you for business; meaning, you have to be clear about your marketing strategy.

The way to do this is to look closely at your target market, dust off your market research from the idea-and-business-plan stage of your business development and come up with a solid plan that tells you the answers to the following.

WHO IS YOUR CUSTOMER?

What is their age, sex, profession, hobbies and income level and, more importantly, where do they live? You should already have discovered this from your market research, but it's vital to know this verbatim and to be clear about it in your mind, otherwise you may find yourself telling the wrong people about your business. For example, if you're an exclusive holiday firm and you choose to advertise in parenting centres and places where children congregate, you may be selling five-star holidays to families who can only afford B&B rates, or to childcarers like nannies and child-minders and not to actual parents.

WHERE DO THEY SHOP?

Again, this information should be in your market research and customer profile, so refer to it to help you to work out where your marketing budget is best spent. Everyone may be online shopping but do your customers want to buy your product or service online or in person? For example, you may have an amazing product or service for the over-sixties that you're selling at a fantastic price on a website, but if your customers are not Internet savvy they won't be able to find you. This means that you would be better off spending your marketing budget elsewhere and going out into the world and drumming up trade yourself rather than having a state-of-the-art website designed for you.

WHAT WOULD GRAB YOUR CUSTOMER'S ATTENTION?

Think about what entices you to buy when you're out shopping. Put yourself in the shoes of your customer and ask yourself, 'If I was shopping, what would make me stop and take notice of this product/service?' A discount? A promotion where you offer something alongside your product? A certain amount of kudos attached to your product? Or even a taster freebie? The answer to these questions will give you an idea of the type of marketing you need to do.

Don't be fooled into thinking that just because you're a start-up Kitchen Table Tycoon you don't have to focus on marketing. Even if you can't afford to go down the advertising route, and want word of mouth (also known as viral marketing) to propel you forwards, you have to have a marketing plan. The following are all ways you can get your business known.

Leaflets and brochures

Producing leaflets and/or brochures is a good way to present your product or service to customers, especially if you have a range of products. Shop around for a low print rate and work out if you're better off posting the leaflets/brochures to prospective customers or leaving them in good locations where a prospective customer might notice them.

Press releases

Time your service, product launch or a promotion to co-incide with a related event; for example, if you're selling chocolates, think about tying it in with Easter or Valentine's Day. If you're setting yourself up as a home cleaning service, tie yourself in with a study on dust mites or launch yourself in spring with a spring-cleaning campaign, and send a press release about yourself to your local paper, magazines and free newsletters (see page 182 for more on this).

Word of mouth

Make full use of viral marketing. Get your customers to spread the word if they are happy with your service. Also ask them for a quote or review of your product and post it on your website or as a press release. Better still, tell good customers to pass it on to their friends and/or give discounts for referrals.

A website

These days the Internet is a very professional place to be, which means the days of DIY sites has long gone. If your idea is to use your website as a calling card for your business or a point of sale, be business savvy and ask a professional to design it for you. Not only so that your site will look professional and be grammatically correct (there's nothing more off-putting to customers than bad spelling), but also so that it will have what's known as good user-ability; that is, your customers (the users), will be able to see your website on the first page of results when they Google you and be able to work their way around your site easily and be able to view and understand what you sell in a limited amount of time. This is vital because if potential customers can't immediately identify how to buy from you or even find you when they do an Internet search, you'll lose them and never get them back again.

To find out if your marketing strategy is working for you, always ask customers how they heard about you and measure the hits as well as sales on your website. Finally, be sure to start a mailing list – this enables you to contact customers for repeat business and to tell them about new promotions and sales.

PR – public relations

Don't assume that you always have to pay to promote your business. The most influential media coverage is editorial, not advertising, which you do not pay for. Learn how to write a press release: come up with a good story, and send it to the relevant press and broadcast contacts for your industry or locality. If you get the story right you can secure a fantastic response.

'Editorial is a cheap form of publicity, if you can get it. It's not only better than paying out for an advert, but if it happens over and over, it can lead to sales, as it puts you firmly in the mind of the public. The trick is to place yourself in the right publication for your customers and to use yourself as the "face" of the business. This means that if you're a shy type of person, it's time to take a deep breath and put on a public confident persona. This is because to make PR work for you, you have to be good at being a spokesperson for your business, as well as someone who can think laterally and come up with good angles that tie in with your product or service (if you're no good at the latter you could always use some of your start-up budget to hire a PR).'

Helen Wooldridge, Cuddledry

How to write press releases

The idea is to get the press interested in your business with a related news story. To achieve this, read the papers every day and keep an eye open for good links to your product, and when you see an angle jump on it. For example, if you know that Green Earth Day is coming up and you sell eco-friendly nappies, send a catchy press release to your local paper that tells them:

➤ How many disposable nappies are used each year and how many end up in landfill sites; how landfill sites are running out.

➤ How your business offers an eco-friendly alternative.

➤ Where people can find you.

➤ Your details, so that the relevant media can contact you for quotes.

If you read that a certain celebrity is worried about a skin rash and you sell a product that deals with that, write a press release that starts with her quote (you don't need permission if you're using a direct quote but don't suggest she uses your product), and then state how many people get rashes, and finally explain how they can all solve the problem by using your product.

By timing a launch, or coming up with a promotion or story to coincide with a related local or national event, or a news story, or by making yourself an expert in a particular field, you could well end up with some excellent press coverage that would be worth thousands in advertising and bring you some great sales.

FOR A GOOD PRESS RELEASE:

➤ It should be no longer than a page in length.

➤ All details must be correct.

➤ Your details should be listed.

➤ Your claims must be backed up.

➤ A sample of the product or service should be enclosed.

➤ Everything must be spelled correctly.

EDITORIAL

If, however, you can't tie your product or service into a newsworthy story, try to look at your business objectively. Step back and think about what your news story is: have you recently landed a big account or reached some sort of anniversary? Or is your own story newsworthy in some way? If so, send out a press release about this and suggest an editorial piece about your business (it can help to send a sample of your product and a good professionally taken portrait of yourself).

If that angle doesn't work for you, enter yourself for as many business awards as possible, as it will not only up your profile if you win but will also give you a ready-made PR opportunity. Finally, if you can think of nothing else, send out a press release about your launch; make it big and add a promotion, then offer yourself up as the spokesperson. Remember: you're there to promote your business, so make sure that whenever you do PR, you:

1. **Look the part** Be groomed – it says a million good things about your business.

2. **Be informed** Having the right information at your fingertips spells 'expert' to the press.

3. **Mention your company** It's the whole aim of your PR, so don't be modest or embarrassed about promoting yourself – you can't afford to be, if you want customers!

Networking

'Due to my professional background I'm lucky that I know a lot about marketing, but I do miss someone to bounce ideas off, so my next step is to find a "business angel" and join a women's business network.'
Justina Perry, MamaBabyBliss

You may hate the idea of networking, especially if you have never had to do it before, but as a small business owner it can be a vital tool in helping your business – and it will also help you grow as a business owner. By being open to new contacts and taking a real interest in other business owners you'll find that opportunities will suddenly spring out of nowhere. In fact, research by the US Bureau of Labor shows that 70 per cent of job opportunities are found through networking, and a study of 500 business owners in Europe said that networking was one of the most important factors in their career success. Network correctly and you can increase your contact base, find a mentor, gain business knowledge and get some vital support.

Basically, there are two main ways to network, depending on where you're based and what your business does. If you're in a city or a fairly large town, or dependent on local customers, look for local networking opportunities that not only open up new avenues for business but also offer you working friendships and the chance to get to know your fellow local business owners. If you're not based near a networking group then consider an online network. These are easy to find (see Resources) and offer a large variety of opportunities to do all of the above via forums, online workshops and chat rooms.

Many Kitchen Table Tycoons shrink from networking and handing out their business card because of a lack of confidence and embarrassment, in the same way that they find setting a price and shouting about their business difficult. Yet, putting yourself out there is vital if you want to be successful. The way to do this effectively at a networking event is to:

➤ Have a couple of sentences at the ready that adequately describe your business in a positive light, but don't go into a sales pitch.

➤ Be clear about what you want to get out of networking – more contacts, friends, help, a mentor – and at the end of the networking event make sure you have reached your objective.

➤ Choose your events with care. Is the angle of the networking group right for you and your business? Are you meeting people you want to connect with?

➤ Remind yourself that you have a great idea to sell, and that when you're networking you're not only doing it for yourself but for your business and your family.

➤ Tell yourself that you are as valid as anyone else out there.

➤ Circulate, and don't just stick to the first person you meet.

➤ Be genuinely interested in people, not just in what they may be able to do for you. Also, think about what you may be able to do for them.

➤ Have your business card at the ready and don't be afraid to offer it or ask for someone else's.

➤ Within the following 24 hours, follow up and contact any friendship or business opportunity you make.

➤ Finally, don't be shy – if you don't ask you don't get!

Don't get stuck in start-up mode

'My long-term aim with these businesses is to build them up
and then sell them at their peak, so that I can have a passive
income for life. This way I know that at some point I won't have
to work and can just be with my kids.'
Amanda Tsinonis, SAReunited and Yesnomaybe

Once you're up and running it can be hard to see past the
day-to-day running of your business and focus on future
plans for growth, yet this is vital if you want your business to
survive. The great thing about being a Kitchen Table Tycoon
and starting small is that your customer base should enable
you to see very clearly what direction you could potentially
move into. This means that within a few months of trading
you should be able to see if you have overestimated the size
of your market and what you need to do to rectify this, or
where you need to focus your attention for future business.
For example, what new markets could you venture into or
what's really selling from your product range or services, and
what isn't?

The trick is to be aware of what's happening from day one
by making yourself take notice of the bigger picture, which
means paying attention to your sales and your cash flow. This
not only helps you to avoid becoming complacent but it also
helps keep you energised about your business.

Also, be aware that even if you're doing amazingly well,
although you need to grow to survive this doesn't necessarily
mean you have to expand so that you need shop or office
premises, or employees. Expansion could simply mean that
you get a business partner or increase output in one area of

your business. It's up to you to decide how big you would like to become or how small you want to stay.

After all, not every company is destined to become a potential global brand or a franchised company (this is where you, the owner, become a franchisor and people pay you for the exclusive right to use your brand name, technology or products as well as your business model and run the business as you would for an agreed period). What's more, not every company has to have a turnover of billions in order to be deemed successful. Sometimes expanding means simply opening your business to other opportunities, such as the mobile spa company MamaBabyBliss, which has branched out from beauty treatments for mothers and babies into spa products, or the website company SAReunited, a site for finding old friends, which has set up a sister site for dating. Expansion can also means diversifying what you have to offer so that you take your initial idea of, say, arranging baby-friendly holiday accommodation in France (Tots to France) to arranging baby-friendly accommodation in Italy, Spain and beyond.

ARE YOU READY TO EXPAND?

Whatever area you decide to expand into it's important to make sure that you can finance your expansion; meaning, before you grow, know where you will get the money to pay for the additional equipment/products/costs that you will need to expand and that you can afford to do this. Also, be wary of promising what you can't deliver. It's great if a chain of shops comes to you with an order for 200,000 products, but before you sign on the dotted line be sure that you have the cash flow to manufacture and deliver this amount of goods.

If you are going to expand, be ready to delegate parts of your business to others, rather than doing it all yourself. The business may be your baby, but expansion means getting help. Consider employing people on a freelance basis or going into business with a partner who has differing talents to your own, or even think about hiring an employee. Whichever direction you decide on, make sure it's somewhere you truly want to go, by rewriting your business plan, looking closely at the financial figures and going over your goals, aims and objectives from Chapters 1 and 2. After all, most growth will take you away from your initial reasons for becoming a Kitchen Table Tycoon. Do you want this, and are you ready for this? Only you can say.

KITCHEN TABLE TYCOON PROFILE
Lucy Lyons and Brett Tyne
Business: Wilbur and Gussie – luxury handbags

'Brett and I have been friends since we went to school together, and in 2004 we were both at a crossroads in our careers. I didn't want to juggle the corporate life with having babies, so I left my job as a fashion buyer for Disney to think of something new. Brett was in New York working as a film producer's assistant at the time, but came home to the UK and suggested we hatch a plan for a small business idea together.

One day we were randomly browsing in a fabric shop looking at row upon row of beautiful silk when the idea to make bags came to us. We couldn't shake the idea off and spent the next few months living in fabric stores and talking about what we could design and create. Our best-selling style is actually based on a clutch bag Brett's grandmother swore by – it's a timeless design, which is the aim for all our bags, and would work with something casual as well as with something head-turning.

When we started we purposely decided to start small, as we didn't want to risk too much. So we each put in £10,000 and went off to trade shows to look at the thousands of companies who produce bags. We knew we had to make a sound decision and choose the right manufacturer, so we became slaves to details, analysing everything from prints to fine stitching, and finally found a factory in Barcelona that could fulfil everything we wanted.

After a year of endless cups of tea at the kitchen table, where we scribbled down ideas, we were ready to show our products to buyers. We signed up for a stall at London Fashion Week and, to our surprise, found a level of interest that we couldn't have dreamed of. Due to that we are now one of the key brands in Fortnum and Mason; we also sell in Harrods, plus Henri Bendel – the legendary Fifth Avenue boutique. Doing a deal with them was a massive thrill and they now order hundreds of bags from us.

The hub of our working day is sitting at my big kitchen table, where designs are dreamed up, fabrics chosen and business decisions made. Since I am a mum of three, my work is UK-based, whereas Brett handles all the long-distance travelling. Wherever we are we speak every day without fail and three times a week we meet to talk shop, if Brett isn't travelling, usually with toddlers weaving around our legs. We also go shopping for fabrics and to talk through ideas. It sounds glamorous, but it's worth knowing that until recently we made our deliveries using the bus because setting up a courier account seemed like an extravagance.

The downside is that because it's our own business it can be emotionally exhausting; when I was pregnant with my third baby I thought it would break us, and, like a coward, I left telling Brett until the last minute. On the other hand our best decisions have been to take on a PR company to raise our media profile, putting in the legwork to find the right manufacturer and showing off our designs at London Fashion Week to make people aware that we were out there.

Best of all, we work well as a team: we're not afraid to be frank with each other and we anchor each other, which means that we make fewer mistakes. Plus, our families are right behind us, although naming our company was a bone of contention, as we named it after my cat Wilbur and Brett's terrier Gussie. My mum was mortified, saying it didn't sound like a label for exquisite handbags, as for my husband, he is simply baffled by the obsession women have with handbags!'

KITCHEN TABLE TYCOON PROFILE

Freya Bletsoe

Business: Homefinder UK Ltd – a property location company that is currently the only endorsed firm of property finders to work for the Professional Footballers Association, finding homes for their footballers when they move. They also offer a 'sell your house for free' service

'I started Homefinder UK Ltd from home because the cost of taking an office at first was huge. Plus, it was very convenient to work from home, as I have three children and one of them at that point wasn't in school full time. Also, I felt that if a garage was good enough for the lads from Google then the kitchen table was good enough for me!

Previously, I had worked for companies such as L'Oreal, and worked as a temp when my first child was a young baby. I worked in customer service and accounts for most of my career, but it was by chance that I got into the property industry. I had an inheritance and although it wasn't thousands it was a lot, and my husband Steve and I thought: well, we can either take some time off and really enjoy this money on a one-off long holiday or we can invest it in property and our future.

So that's what we did, we bought a property, did it up and sold it for a profit, then we took the money and put it into the next house. Soon our friends were looking to buy their first houses and they were coming to us for advice on house buying. Then we started to get calls from friends of friends asking for help and that's when we knew we were on to a good business idea!

To secure funding for the business we took all the money we had built up in investment properties, sold our house and moved from an eight-bedroom house in Wales to a three-bedroom house in Yorkshire. We also raided our other savings and paid for our general living expenses on credit cards (not the best solution I'll readily admit!), as well as having a couple of loans from family members, too. Now the company is starting to grow, we have attracted a significant six-figure sum from a consortium of investors who are looking to push the franchising side of the company forward, so it's paid off.

The highs have been when the investors came on board and when we got our first franchisee to sign up, but the lows were when the bank manager wanted to close our account for the sake of £200 in excess of our overdraft facility! He actually said that he could help us with a short-term loan if he "got" what we did, or if we were a green-grocer … but because we had no other company to benchmark ourselves against he wasn't willing to help us out. So, being leaders in a new field has sometimes been very hard. If no one's gone before you then you definitely need an entrepreneurial bank manager or investor to see the potential value in your company, and you certainly need them to be willing to take a risk with you – not the easiest thing to get a bank manager to do!

It really wasn't easy to take the franchise beyond the "light bulb" stage. Firstly, this style of business is still relatively new in the UK (not so much in the US), so there was very little information about it out there – and I had to convince Steve that it was the way to go with the business. I think he was convinced only when people kept asking him at networking events if the company was a franchise that he'd bought, so this was the point when he became convinced that we should franchise. As for the Sell For Free service that we offer, that was very much consumer-requirement driven. When people discovered that we found homes for people, we started getting more and more people offering us their homes "just to see" if any of our clients might be interested in buying them. After a while we had so many people offering us properties that we launched Sell For Free as a fully fledged service, and it's just gone from strength to strength. So, a lot of the ideas have either come from the seed of something else or out of necessity from having to bootstrap in the beginning.

My tip to other mums wanting to start up from home is to just do it! It's that simple: find a corner of the house to call your own and it doesn't matter how humble your beginnings are – if you want to make it big, over time you will find a way to do so. On the other hand, if you want to keep it simple and don't want to grow so much, then working from home will definitely give you the flexibility to do that.

My best advice for anyone starting at their kitchen table is to try to keep home and work separate, but most of all enjoy the freedom it brings with it. My family has benefited hugely from me working from home. It has given me a degree of flexibility to be able to pick my children up from school and

now the knock-on effect is that our staff benefit, too – as
we actively promote home working for a percentage of our
staff and our franchisees. We know they value that freedom
and flexibility – just as we did when we were working from
the kitchen table. Indeed, I do sometimes still work from the
same kitchen table now when the mood takes me to work
from home!'

KITCHEN TABLE TYCOON PROFILE

Becky DeYoung

Business: DeYoung's Fore Seasons – a gourmet spice company

'For over 15 years, my husband Mark worked in the kitchens throughout the Metro Detroit area and it was there that he found a need for adding extra flavour to the average main entrée and side dish. He experimented until he achieved the final blend of 18 robust herbs and spices. In 1999, a family member suggested making the secret blend and selling it, and we called it DeYoung's Fore Seasons Gourmet Spice Blend. It was originally created to be a financial security blanket for our future family, but soon after the company's launch we found the future was a lot sooner than later and William was born in 2000 and Gregory in 2001. We then decided to sideline the spice business until the children went to school, since Mark and I already had full-time jobs.

In January of 2005, I decided to leave my outside sales job because of the long commute and lack of quality family time – also, missing the small milestones of my boys' lives made me unhappy. I tried looking for a new career with a more flexible schedule, but with no success, so I decided it was time to reintroduce DeYoung's Fore Seasons. Mark continued to hold a full-time restaurant management position, while I did all aspects of the business.

In the beginning I knew nothing about website design or business in general but, through hours of Internet research and tutorials, I taught myself everything I needed to know.

I started by joining a small Internet group called BuyMichiganProducts.com, which supported Michigan's small businesses. Then I met a counsellor from Michigan State University who told me of a programme that helps agricultural entrepreneurs develop their businesses, utilising all the resources from the university. For a small nominal fee I could access any service – from help with the business-plan process to finding dietary services – and since joining I have a much better understanding of what I wanted from our product.

Then I started visiting stores. My first hurdle was that a similar product hit the shelves two weeks before I began' and the creator happened to be an older man with a reputation in the restaurant business. Thankfully, I had already built some strong relationships through my old job in sales, and when retailers learned it was my own personal product they gave me a chance. I looked at the other product as healthy competition, but after a year the first product disappeared off the shelves. Now, two years later, we are in 50 stores throughout Michigan and have online purchasing coast to coast.

When I started this empowering journey, I emailed, mailed and called every morning-radio show, the local TV stations, hometown newspapers, and Internet sites, etc. Oprah probably wonders what happened to me, because for almost six months I emailed her daily. I also gave packages of our blends to friends and family to start handing out. I also did, and still do, a lot of trade shows and festivals to get samples into the mouths of a captive audience. It helps to put a face behind the blend. Being six foot one, outspoken and large framed – I'm not soon forgotten.

Through dedication and basic pestering, we have now been mentioned on three radio stations, had six cooking segments on local TV shows, three newspaper articles, and had two separate articles on MSNBC affiliates, and, as a result the orders came pouring in from coast to coast.

Although I love working from home, juggling the spice business, two boys, a puppy and a husband who suffers from four herniated discs, it is definitely hard work. My average day starts at 4.30 am (the Internet never sleeps – thank God for technology). I check and answer emails, read website usage reports and look for possible avenues of marketing. My boys then wake up between 6.00 and 7.00 am and they usually allow me to work until lunch, and then it's outside with them for the rest of the day. Store visits, meetings and finding new accounts are done on Mark's day off, and weekends are saved for trade shows and festivals.

My best tip for other women who want to embrace their dream is to believe in yourself. Put your heart and soul into what you're doing because no one is going to do it for you. Overall, although I have my good days and bad days it's been worth it. I answer to no one but myself. If I want to take the morning or afternoon off, I don't have to ask anyone, and whatever happens I would much rather be at my home office than behind a steering wheel stuck in the afternoon traffic.'

The rollercoaster ride of being a Kitchen Table Tycoon

Lack of money, bad concentration, household chores, kid problems and cash-flow worries are some of the common woes that plague the Kitchen Table Tycoon and are likely to keep you up at night. Which is why if you're going to work from home you need to be prepared to be stressed most of the time, because running a successful business out of your home and scheduling your work around your kids is difficult, and there's no getting away from that. However, it's an option that can heap a multitude of benefits on your children's lives and yours, so it's worth the hassle and the strain.

To help get the balance in your life right, and not find yourself working until the early hours, surviving on a few hours' sleep a night, you have to learn to identify your stress triggers early on and deal with them before they get out of control.

Key stress points for many Kitchen Table Tycoons are:

Multitasking Trying to do too many things for work and home at the same time, within a limited amount of time, spells trouble.
Stress busters Hire a cleaner, hire freelance help, and get a babysitter for two hours.

Guilt Feeling guilty for not spending enough time with the kids or on the business.
Stress buster Remind yourself that working on your business is for your kids as well as you.

Worrying about money Constantly thinking about whether your business will make you a living and whether you can cope until the money starts coming in.

Stress buster It's totally normal and, sadly, doesn't go away. When you're in business for yourself money is always a headache, even when you're successful.

The answer to the stresses of being a Kitchen Table Tycoon is to (a) accept that you're going to be stressed; and (b) be someone who can ask for and accept help. It might sound ridiculous to say that you must accept being stressed, but trying to avoid it when it's a natural by-product of being your own boss only leads to more stress. Instead, see the pressure as a motivating tool. Also, remember that you can't do it all yourself, so ask for help, admit you're struggling when you feel you can't cope and accept any offers to help you out.

At the same time, set firm boundaries and create separate schedules on paper for business and family responsibilities. This means that when you are in work mode, work – and don't be distracted by the kids (although one of the benefits of being at home is being able to admire a piece of art work or stop for a quick cuddle). When in mum mode, switch off the computer and turn your BlackBerry to silent, and don't be distracted by texts and emails. It's hard to stop working when you're running your own business, but keep reminding yourself that your business will suffer if you're exhausted, and your kids won't want you at home if the only reaction they can get from you is an irritable and frustrated one.

Above all, create a routine every day so that you all know when you're working, when you're being mum, and when you have some time alone, so that everyone understands what's expected of them. Don't be like my friend, who tells her kids she's working and then takes business calls while cleaning the cooker, so they are always unsure of what mode she is in. If you're going to work from home, something's got to give and this is usually domestic stuff.

Finally, in between being a mother and a Kitchen Table Tycoon, be sure to schedule in some time just to be you, as well as some time off (remember: no one needs to work seven days a week, and those who do, choose to do it). Running your own business does require sacrifices, but you time and relaxation time are also vital parts of who you are, and need to be scheduled in if you don't want to run the risk of exhaustion.

If you feel guilty about having some time for yourself, remind yourself that the best part of running your own business is that you get to do it on your own terms, which means you set the schedule and you dictate when it's work time and when it isn't. Letting work take over your life goes against improving the quality of your family life, and you need to remind yourself that this was one of the main reasons why you went into business for yourself in the first place.

Get the balance right and you'll find that you'll reap rewards, not only professionally but personally, too, which means being one of the lucky ones who gets to do something she loves for a living but doesn't have to do it at the expense of her family.

Appendix

KITCHEN TABLE TYCOONS

Janine Allis – Boost Juice: www.boostjuicebars.com

Danielle Ayotte and Julie Dix – Taggies: www.taggies.com

Jenni Baxter – Bluex2 Web Design: www.bluex2.com

Freya Bletsoe – Homefinder UK: www.homefinderuk.com

Barbara Cox – Nutrichef: www.nutrichef.co.uk

Beverley Daniels – photography:
www.beverleydanielsphotography.com

Becky DeYoung – DeYoung's Fore Seasons:
www.deyoungsforeseasons.com

Nadine Hill – The Dream PA: www.thedreampa.co.uk

Karen Lumb – Alleyn Park Garden Centre:
www.alleynpark.co.uk

Lucy Lyons and Brett Tyne – Wilbur and Gussie:
www.wilburandgussie.com

Sandra McClumpha – Fake Bake UK: www.fakebake.co.uk

Louise Millar – Memoir Publishing:
www.memoirpublishing.com

Felicity Morgan – The Organic Flower Company:
www.tofc.co.uk

Justina Perry – MamaBabyBliss: www.mamababybliss.com

Louise Potts – Naked Body Care: www.nakedbodycare.
co.uk

Sally Preston – Babylicious: www.babylicious.co.uk

Melissa Roske – Wheels in Motion Coaching:
www.wheelsinmotioncoaching.com

Wendy Shand – Tots to France: www.totstofrance.co.uk

Melissa Talago – Peekaboo Communications:
www.peekaboocoms.co.uk

Rachael Talpin – AboutMyArea and Mums In Control:
www.aboutmyarea.com www.mumsincontrol.com

Amanda Tsinonis – SAReunited and Yesnomaybe:
www.sareunited.com www.yesnomayb.co.uk

Leila Wilcox – Halo 'n' Horns: www.halogb.co.uk

Helen Wooldridge – Cuddledry: www.cuddledry.com

Resources

UK

Business Help

Aurora Women's Network: www.network.auroravoice.com
Europe's leading businesswomen's network, providing
events, training, online communities and resources for
accelerating women-owned businesses from start-up
to growth.

Business Link Helpline: www.businesslink.gov.uk
All you need to know about setting up a business.
Tel: 0845 600 9 006

Business Plan Help: www.businessplanhelp.co.uk

Business Eye: www.businesseye.org.uk
Whether you have a new idea, are an established company,
a sole trader or an employer of hundreds, Business Eye
Wales can put you in contact with support from the public,
private or voluntary sectors.

Bytestart – small business portal: www.bytestart.co.uk

Everywoman: www.everywoman.co.uk
An online resource for female entrepreneurs. Small-business funding, grants for women in business, female career advice and mentoring.

Equal Opportunities Commission: www.eoc.org.uk

Institute of Business Advisers: www.iba.org.uk
Mentors, advisers and consulting help.

Mother@Work: www.motheratwork.co.uk
Information on everything from business to finance to a work–life balance.

Mumpreneurs: www.mumpreneurs.com
Support, ideas and inspiration for women who combine running their own business with motherhood.

National Federation of Enterprise Agencies: www.nfea.com
Find your local enterprise agency.

Princes Trust: www.princes-trust.org.uk
Help and loans for your business if you are aged 18–30.

Prowess: www.prowess.org.uk
The UK association of organisations and individuals who support women to start and grow businesses in the UK.

Scottish Businesswomen: www.scottishbusinesswomen.com
Provides information and advice to help women develop their business ideas.

Shell-Livewire: www.shell-livewire.org
Business start-up help for 16–30-year-olds.

Small Business: www.smallbusiness.co.uk
Help for all small businesses, including banking, legal
services, starting up and so on.

Small business service: www.sbs.gov.uk

Start-up Business Help: www.startups.co.uk

The Bag Lady: www.the-bag-lady.co.uk
A leading online directory and international trading portal
for women in business.

WIRE: www.wireuk.org
For rural women business owners with up-to-date
information, advice and research.

Women at Work: www.womenatwork.co.uk
A comprehensive database of women running small
businesses or working for themselves in a wide range
of occupations.

Finance for start-up organisations

Advantage Business Angels:
www.advantagebusinessangels.com
Offers help to small to medium enterprises to find funding
through business angels.

Bank of Scotland –Women in Business: www.
bankofscotlandbusiness.co.uk/womeninbusiness
Provides top tips, guides to starting a business, research
extracts, useful links and free downloads of the *Big Fish*
magazine for women in business.

British Business Angels Association: www.bbaa.org.uk
BBAA brings together investors with commercial
experience and companies looking for development capital.

British Venture Capital Association: www.bvca.co.uk
The BVCA represents most major sources of venture
capital in the UK.

Community Development Finance Association:
www.cdfa.org.uk
The CDFA can put you in touch with local providers of
loans for a small business and social enterprises.

j4b: www.j4b.co.uk
The site allows quick and simple searches of a regularly
updated database of business grants and loans.

AUSTRALIA

AusIndustry: www.ozsmallbiz.net
AusIndustry is the Australian government's business
programme delivery division in the Department of
Industry, Tourism and Resources, and it provides a range
of incentives to support business innovation.

Business Enterprise Centres: www.beca.org.au
www.business.gov.au
Offers you simple and convenient access to all the
government information, transactions and services you
need. It's a whole-of-government service providing
essential information on planning, starting and running
your business.

Flying Solo: www.flyingsolo.com.au
Flying Solo has been created for the fastest-growing
segment of the business community: the solo business
owner. The site includes resources and articles giving
guidance on the practicalities of operating a solo business.

Small Business Support Network: www.ozsmallbiz.net

Smart Start: www.ipaustralia.gov.au/smartstart/index.htm
Protecting your intellectual property in Australia.

NEW ZEALAND

Business Mentors New Zealand:
www.businessmentor.org.nz
Approximately 1,300 volunteer mentors are provided by
Business Mentors New Zealand to offer the extensive range
of business knowledge, skills and experience required. You
can apply for the help of a business mentor.

New Zealand Business Information Zone: www.biz.org.nz

New Zealand trade and enterprise: www.nzte.govt.nz

Small Business Enterprise Centres: www.sbecnz.org.nz
Community-based organisations located in city and
rural areas with central coordination by Small Business
Enterprise Centres of New Zealand Inc.

SOUTH AFRICA

Business Women's Association: www.bwasa.co.za

Department of Trade and Industry South Africa:
www.dti.gov.za

New business help SA:
www.southafrica.info/doing_business/trends/newbusiness

CANADA

Business start-up assistance: www.bsa.cbsc.org

Canada Business Service Centre: www.cbsc.org
Help for start-ups in Ontario.

Canada Revenue Agency (CRA):
www.cra-arc.gc.ca/tax/business/sme/menu-e.html
Overview of your obligations and entitlements under
Canadian laws.

Small Business Resources: www.sbinfocanada.about.com

USA

Entrepreneur: www.entrepreneur.com

Home Based Working Mums: www.hbwm.com

Inc.com – resource site for entrepreneurs: www.inc.com

Mompreneursonline.com: www.mompreneursonline.com

National Association of Women Business Owners:
www.nawbo.org

Score: www.score.org
Help for small businesses.

Trademark: www.trademark.com

USA Small Business Administration: www.sba.gov

Welcome Business: www.welcomebusiness.com
Small business portal.

Index